T0346094

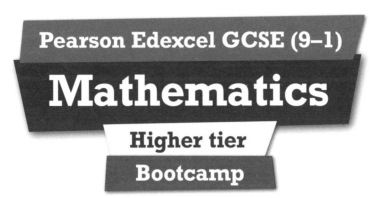

**Pearson Edexcel GCSE (9–1)**

# Mathematics

## Higher tier

### Bootcamp

Series consultant: Harry Smith
Author: Harry Smith

## Also available to support your revision:

Revise GCSE Study Skills Guide    9781292318875

The **Revise GCSE Study Skills Guide** is full of tried-and-trusted hints and tips for how to learn more effectively. It gives you techniques to help you achieve your best – throughout your GCSE studies and beyond!

Revise GCSE Revision Planner    9781292318868

The **Revise GCSE Revision Planner** helps you to plan and organise your time, step-by-step, throughout your GCSE revision. Use this book and wall chart to mastermind your revision.

For the full range of Pearson revision titles across KS2, 11+, KS3, GCSE, Functional Skills, AS/A Level and BTEC visit: www.pearsonschools.co.uk/revise

# Welcome to Bootcamp

GCSE Maths Bootcamp is designed to help you squeeze the maximum amount of useful revision into the minimum amount of time. This book contains 30 short workouts, which can each be completed in about 20 minutes. Finish the whole book and you can be exam-fit in just 10 hours!

Check out these great features that appear on each workout.

Quick warm-ups remind you of the key facts and formulae for this workout.

Use this tracker to check your progress at-a-glance. This is Workout 12, so you are nearly half-way there!

Exam-standard questions so you can be confident you're revising at the right level.

If you need a bit more help, check out these pages in the Pearson Edexcel GCSE Maths Higher Revision Guide.

Super strategies to help you master problem-solving questions.

Get the inside track with these top exam tips from our experts.

Build your confidence with these reps. The first one has been done for you each time.

Tick off each workout once you have finished it.

The scale next to each question tells you how difficult it is. If you are stuck on a tricky question, try coming back to it later.

**Guided**

We've given you a head start on some questions. Look out for this "guided" icon and complete the working to find the correct solution.

# Contents

Aim to spend about 20 minutes on each workout.

You will find answers to the reps questions and full worked solutions to all the exam-style questions at the back of the book. Use them to check your progress.

# Number crunch

## Warm up

✓ The factors of a number divide exactly into it. You can draw a **factor tree** to find the **prime factors** of a number.

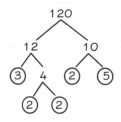

$$120 = 2^3 \times 3 \times 5$$

✓ Use the index laws to simplify powers:

**1** $a^m \times a^n = a^{m+n}$  **4** $a^{-n} = \dfrac{1}{a^n}$

**2** $(a^m)^n = a^{mn}$  **5** $\left(\dfrac{a}{b}\right)^n = \dfrac{a^n}{b^n}$

**3** $\dfrac{a^m}{a^n} = a^{m-n}$  **6** $a^{\frac{1}{n}} = \sqrt[n]{a}$

✓ **Surds** are used to give exact answers to calculations by leaving some values as square roots:

$$\sqrt{ab} = \sqrt{a}\sqrt{b} \qquad \sqrt{\dfrac{a}{b}} = \dfrac{\sqrt{a}}{\sqrt{b}} \qquad \sqrt{a^2 b} = a\sqrt{b}$$

## Reps

**1** Circle any prime factors of the given number in each list.

|     | 12 | 1 | ② | ③ | 4 |
|-----|----|----|----|----|----|
| a   | 20 | 4 | 5 | 10 | 20 |
| b   | 100 | 2 | 5 | 10 | 50 |
| c   | 45 | 3 | 5 | 9 | 15 |

**3** Write as a single power of 5

$5^3 \times 5$  $5^4$

a $5^2 \div 25$  ..................

b $(5^3)^2$  ..................

c $25^5$  ..................

**2** Find the value of

$100^{-\frac{1}{2}}$  $\dfrac{1}{10}$

a $36^{\frac{1}{2}}$  ..................

b $3^4$  ..................

c $8^{-\frac{1}{3}}$  ..................

**4** Match up the equivalent surds.

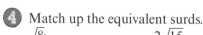

$\sqrt{8}$  $2\sqrt{15}$

$\dfrac{60}{\sqrt{5}}$  $\dfrac{\sqrt{2}}{2}$

$\sqrt{60}$  $2\sqrt{2}$

$\dfrac{1}{\sqrt{2}}$  $12\sqrt{5}$

## Exam practice

**1.** Write 96 as a product of its prime factors.

**(2 marks)**

**Links to:**
Pages 1–3, 12

Remember that these are **non-calculator** questions. Use the index laws to work out the values in stages:

**2.** Find the value of

**(a)** $25^{-\frac{1}{2}}$

**(2 marks)**

$$\left(\frac{8}{27}\right)^{\frac{2}{3}} = \frac{8^{\frac{2}{3}}}{27^{\frac{2}{3}}} = \frac{\left(8^{\frac{1}{3}}\right)^2}{\left(27^{\frac{1}{3}}\right)^2}$$

**(b)** $\left(\frac{8}{27}\right)^{\frac{2}{3}}$

**(2 marks)**

### Problem solved!

To **rationalise a denominator** in the form $a + \sqrt{b}$, multiply the numerator and denominator by $a - \sqrt{b}$

**3.** Show that $\dfrac{\sqrt{12} - 1}{2 + \sqrt{3}}$ can be written in the form $p\sqrt{3} + q$, where $p$ and $q$ are integers.

**(3 marks)**

Work out $(2 + \sqrt{3})(2 - \sqrt{3})$ by expanding the brackets. You can practise this skill in Workout 5.

**Guided**

$$\frac{\sqrt{12} - 1}{2 + \sqrt{3}} = \frac{\left(\sqrt{12} - 1\right)\left(2 - \sqrt{3}\right)}{\left(2 + \sqrt{3}\right)\left(2 - \sqrt{3}\right)}$$

$$= \frac{2\sqrt{12} - \sqrt{12}\sqrt{3} - 2 + \sqrt{3}}{\dots}$$

$$= \dots$$

### Top exam tip!

Learn the squares of 1 to 15, the cubes of 1 to 5 and the corresponding square roots and cube roots.

# 2 Fractions, decimals and percentages

## Warm up

✓ Tips for working with fractions:

| Add or subtract | Multiply | Divide | Mixed numbers |
|---|---|---|---|
| Find equivalent fractions with the same denominator | Multiply the numerators and the denominators | Turn the second fraction upside down then multiply | Write as improper fractions first |

✓ In a **recurring decimal**, the dots tell you which digit or group of digits repeats forever. For example, $0.7\dot{3}\dot{5} = 0.735\,353\,535...$

✓ Use a **multiplier** to find a percentage increase or decrease. Divide by the multiplier to find the original amount.

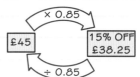

## Reps

**1** Work out

$\frac{1}{5} + \frac{1}{2}$      $\frac{7}{10}$

a $\frac{1}{2} + \frac{1}{4}$ ......................

b $1\frac{1}{2} \times \frac{3}{5}$ ......................

c $\frac{5}{6} \div \frac{3}{4}$ ......................

**2** Circle the largest number in each list.

0.3    $\frac{1}{3}$    0.28    ⓪.4

a 0.24    0.42    $\frac{1}{2}$    $\frac{2}{5}$

b 0.2$\dot{5}$    0.25    0.$\dot{2}\dot{5}$    0.$\dot{2}$

c 0.$\dot{8}$    $\frac{4}{5}$    0.8$\dot{5}$    0.85

**3** Write the correct multiplier.

10% increase      1.1

a 50% increase ......................

b 20% decrease ......................

c 42% decrease ......................

**4** Each amount has been increased by 35%. Find the original amounts.

£270          £200

a 67.5 g ......................

b 2.43 m ......................

c 1350 km ......................

## Exam practice

**1.** Work out $1\frac{1}{4} \times 2\frac{3}{5}$

Give your answer as a mixed number.

**(3 marks)**

**Links to:**
Pages 5, 6, 9, 62, 63

> Convert mixed numbers to fractions:
>
> $$2\frac{3}{5} = \frac{2 \times 5 + 3}{5} = \frac{13}{5}$$

...............

**2.** $x = 0.2\dot{6}$
Prove algebraically that $x$ can be written as $\frac{4}{15}$

**(3 marks)**

> To convert a recurring decimal to a fraction, you multiply by 10, 100 or 1000. Then subtract to remove the recurring part and simplify the fraction.

**Guided**

$$10x = 2.6666\ldots$$
$$100x = \ldots\ldots\ldots$$
$$90x = 100x - 10x$$
$$= \ldots\ldots\ldots$$

$$x = \frac{\ldots\ldots\ldots}{\ldots\ldots\ldots} = \frac{\ldots\ldots\ldots}{\ldots\ldots\ldots}$$

### Problem solved!

**3.** Jaden buys 20 bars of chocolate for a total of £7.95.
She sells all 20 bars for 60p each.
Work out Jaden's percentage profit.

**(3 marks)**

> Read word problems carefully. Here you are asked to find the percentage profit.

### Top exam tip!

> To find a percentage change, you divide the increase or decrease by the **original amount**, then multiply by 100%.

...............%

**Workout 2** ☐

## 3 Estimation and error

### Warm up

✓ The first digit in a number which is not zero is the first **significant figure (s.f.)**. To round a number to 1 significant figure, look at the **next digit**:

- if it is 5 or more, round up       0.0761 rounds to 0.08 to 1 s.f.

- if it is less than 5, round down.   This is the first significant figure.

✓ To estimate an answer to a calculation, round each number to 1 s.f.

✓ You can write an **error interval** for a rounded number. Here is the error interval for 2.90 rounded to 2 decimal places:

This is the **lower bound**. It is the smallest value that will round to 2.90

$2.895 \leqslant x < 2.905$

Use $\leqslant$ for the lower bound and $<$ for the upper bound.

This is the **upper bound**. The value of $x$ must be less than this to round to 2.90

### Reps

**1** Round to 1 significant figure.

2340          2000

a 0.251       ...........................

b 8.70        ...........................

c 345         ...........................

d 0.003 72    ...........................

**2** Each number has been rounded to 1 s.f. Find the upper bound.

0.3          0.35

a 500        ...........................

b 8          ...........................

c 0.002      ...........................

d 0.09       ...........................

**3** Estimate the answer by rounding each number.

$2.1 \times 37$       80

a $5.5 \times 8.9$    ...........................

b $29.3 \div 4.5$     ...........................

c $7.75^2$            ...........................

d $391 \times 0.470$  ...........................

**4** Write the missing number in each error interval.

$5.5 \leqslant x < 6.5$

a $8500 \leqslant x < $ .........................

b .......................... $\leqslant x < 0.75$

c $10.5 \leqslant x < $ .........................

d .......................... $\leqslant x < 3.05$

## Exam practice

**1.** A number, $n$, is rounded to 1 decimal place. The result is 10.5
Write down the error interval for $n$.

**(2 marks)**

You must use inequalities when writing down an error interval.

.....................

**2.** Work out an estimate for

$$\frac{221 \times 5.2}{0.185}$$

**(2 marks)**

Round each number to **1 significant figure**. You can sometimes simplify a fraction calculation by multiplying the top and bottom by 10.

.....................

**3.** A mountain biker completes a course in 17 minutes, correct to the nearest minute. The course is 6.4 km long, correct to 1 decimal place.
Calculate the lower bound of the average speed of the mountain biker. Give your answer in m/s correct to 2 decimal places.

**(3 marks)**

### Problem solved!

If you are **dividing** by a rounded number, then choose the upper bound to make the answer as small as possible.

**Guided**

| | Upper bound | Lower bound |
|---|---|---|
| Distance (m) | 6450 | ..................... |
| Time (s) | ..................... | $16.5 \times 60 = 990$ |

Lower bound for speed

$$= \frac{.....................}{.....................} = .....................$$

..................... m/s

### Top exam tip!

If you are given rounded values in a question, write out the upper and lower bound for each rounded value.

## 4 ⟩ Large and small numbers

✓ Numbers in **standard form** are written in two parts:

A number part which is greater than or equal to 1 and less than 10 ‑‑‑ $2.6 \times 10^9$ ‑‑‑ An integer power of 10

✓ You can enter numbers in standard form into your calculator using the $\times 10^x$ key.

✓ The **product rule** for counting says that if there are $m$ ways to choose one item, and $n$ ways to choose another item, then there are $m \times n$ ways to choose both items.

**Reps**

**1** Write in standard form.

0.0035     $3.5 \times 10^{-3}$

a 29 000     ......................

b 0.05     ......................

c 9 010 000     ......................

d 0.000 06     ......................

**2** Write as an ordinary number.

$1.8 \times 10^5$     180 000

a $6.9 \times 10^{-1}$     ......................

b $8 \times 10^4$     ......................

c $2.03 \times 10^2$     ......................

d $5.5 \times 10^{-3}$     ......................

**3** Find the number of different possible outcomes when each set of spinners is spun.

$3 \times 4 = 12$

a ......................

b ......................

c ......................

## Exam practice

**1.** Work out $(6.5 \times 10^6) \times (2 \times 10^{-13})$.
Give your answer in standard form.

**(2 marks)**

**Guided**

$(6.5 \times 2) \times (10^6 \times \text{.....................})$

$= \text{.....................} \times 10^{\cdots}$

$= \text{.....................} \times 10^{\cdots}$

.........................

> Make sure your final answer is in standard form. This means the first number must be between 1 and 10.

**Links to:**
Pages 8, 13

**2.** Amy needs to choose a starter and a main course at a restaurant. A menu contains 7 different choices of starter and some main course options.
Amy says, 'There are exactly 80 different ways in which I could choose a starter and a main course.'
Is Amy correct? Give a reason for your answer. **(2 marks)**

**Guided**

$\dfrac{80}{7} = $ .........................

...........................................................

## Problem solved!

If there are $n$ starters and $m$ mains, then the total number of different ways of choosing is $n \times m$. Remember that $n$ and $m$ must be integers.

**3.** A combination lock consists of two letters from A to Z, followed by three digits from 0 to 9

Work out the total number of possible combinations. Give your answer in standard form. **(3 marks)**

.........................

> There are 26 possible choices for each letter, and 10 possible choices for each number. Write out the number of combinations as an ordinary number before converting to standard form.

## Top exam tip!

If you are giving answers in standard form, always double check that the number part is greater than or equal to 1 and less than 10.

# 5 ▶ Algebra essentials

## Warm up

✓ You can use the index laws with powers of the same letter:

**1** $a^m \times a^n = a^{m+n}$  **2** $(a^m)^n = a^{mn}$  **3** $\dfrac{a^m}{a^n} = a^{m-n}$

✓ To expand two brackets you can use a grid, or the FOIL method. FOIL stands for **F**irst, **O**utside, **I**nside, **L**ast:

|   | $x$ | $-4$ |
|---|-----|------|
| $x$ | $x^2$ | $-4x$ |
| $3$ | $3x$ | $-12$ |

$$(x + 3)(x - 4) = \overset{F}{x^2} - \overset{O}{4x} + \overset{I}{3x} - \overset{L}{12}$$
$$= x^2 - x - 12$$

✓ Factorising is the opposite of expanding brackets.

✓ To factorise an expression in the form $x^2 + bx + c$ you need to find two numbers which **add up to b**, and which **multiply to make c**.

## Reps

**1** Match the simplified expressions.

$x^2 \times 2xy$     $8x^2y^2$

$4x \times 2xy^2$     $2xy$

$2x^2y \times xy^2$     $2x^3y$

$\dfrac{2x^2y}{x}$     $4x^2y^3$

$x^2y \times 4y^2$     $2x^3y^3$

**2** Find a pair of numbers with the given sum and product.

| Sum | Product | Numbers |
|-----|---------|---------|
| 7 | 12 | 3 and 4 |
| a | 8 | 7 |
| b | 3 | $-4$ |
| c | $-2$ | $-15$ |
| d | $-6$ | 9 |

**3** Expand and simplify

$(x + 1)(x + 3)$    $x^2 + 4x + 3$

a $n(2 + n) + 3n$    .......................

b $(y + 2)(y - 4)$    .......................

c $(3p + 5)(p - 2)$    .......................

d $(x^2 + 1)(x^2 - 1)$    .......................

**4** Factorise

$x^2 + 6x + 5$    $(x + 1)(x + 5)$

a $2x^3 - 4xy$    .......................

b $y^2 - 2y - 3$    .......................

c $3n^2 + 4n + 1$    .......................

d $9a^2 - 4b^2$    .......................

## Exam practice

**Links to:**
Pages 16–18

**1.** Factorise fully                    **(2 marks)**

(a) $4y^2 + 10y$

$$= 2(2y^2 + \text{........}y)$$

$$= \text{........}(2y + \text{........})$$

.........................

(b) $2x^2 + 5x - 3$                 **(3 marks)**

.........................

The first term is $2x^2$. This means your factorised expression will look like $(2x\text{........})(x\text{........})$.

Try different pairs of numbers with a product of $-3$.

**2.** Expand and simplify

(a) $4(x - 1) + 5(2x + 3)$          **(2 marks)**

.........................

(b) $(n + 2)(n + 5)^2$              **(3 marks)**

This is a product of 3 brackets. The highest power of $n$ in your expanded expression will be $n^3$.

$$= n(n + 5)^2 + \text{........}(n + 5)^2$$

$$= n(n^2 + 10n + 25) + \text{.................................}$$

$$= \text{.................................................}$$

$$= n^3 + \text{........}n^2 + \text{........}n + \text{........}$$

.........................

### Problem solved!

Don't panic if what you have to show doesn't seem to be related to the diagram!

1. Multiply the sides

2. Set that expression equal to 8

3. Simplify

**3.** The area of this rectangle is $8\,\text{cm}^2$.

$x + 1$ cm

$x + 6$ cm

Show that $x^2 + 7x - 2 = 0$          **(3 marks)**

### Top exam tip!

When you are working with algebra, write down every line of your working.

**Workout 5**

# 6 Formulae and equations

## Warm up

✓ You can **solve** a linear equation by rearranging the equation so the unknown is on its own on one side. Follow these steps when solving a linear equation:

| Multiply through to get rid of any fractions | ⟹ | Expand any brackets and simplify | ⟹ | Add or subtract number parts and multiples of x | ⟹ | Divide by the number in front of x to get it on its own |
|---|---|---|---|---|---|---|

✓ A formula is a rule used to work out the value of one letter by **substituting** the values of other letters.

$$7x + 10y \qquad\qquad 2x + 1 = 9 \qquad\qquad F = ma$$

This **expression** has two **terms** and no = sign.

This **equation** has one **unknown** and an = sign.

This **formula** has **more than one unknown** and an = sign.

## Reps

**1** Solve

$4x + 3 = 19 \qquad x = 4$

a $10x - 10 = 60 \qquad x = \ldots\ldots$

b $2x + 1 = 6x - 9 \qquad x = \ldots\ldots$

c $8 - 8x = 20 - 2x \qquad x = \ldots\ldots$

d $\dfrac{x}{6} + \dfrac{x}{3} = 5 \qquad x = \ldots\ldots$

**2** Write 'expression', 'equation' or 'formula'.

$4a + 2b \qquad$ expression

a $10x^2 - 1 \qquad \ldots\ldots$

b $p = 2q + 1 \qquad \ldots\ldots$

c $x = 2x - 5 \qquad \ldots\ldots$

d $2y = 8 \qquad \ldots\ldots$

**3** Substitute into the formula

$$F = \dfrac{x^2 - 2y}{z}$$

|   | $x$ | $y$ | $z$ | $F$ |
|---|---|---|---|---|
|   | 4 | 2 | 3 | 4 |
| a | 2 | 1 | 1 |   |
| b | 5 | 5 | 5 |   |
| c | 10 | 10 | −4 |   |

**4** Make $Q$ the subject of each formula.

$$P = 10Q + R \qquad Q = \dfrac{P - R}{10}$$

a $P = Q + 50 \qquad \ldots\ldots\ldots$

b $P = \dfrac{Q + 1}{5} \qquad \ldots\ldots\ldots$

c $P = 2QR + 5 \qquad \ldots\ldots\ldots$

## Exam practice

**Links to:**
Pages 19–21, 46

**Guided**

**1.** Find the area of this square. **(4 marks)**

$3x - 5 = x + 2$

$3x = x +$ .........

.........$x =$ .........

$x =$ .........

Side length = .........

So area = ......... cm$^2$

.................... cm$^2$

$3x - 5$ cm

$x + 2$ cm

### Problem solved!

You can form your own equation and solve it to find the value of $x$. Use the fact that all four sides of a square are the same length. Make sure your final answer is the **area** of the square, not the value of $x$.

**2.** Solve $\dfrac{2x + 1}{3} = x - 7$ **(3 marks)**

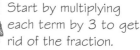

Start by multiplying each term by 3 to get rid of the fraction.

$x =$ ....................

**3.** The following formula can be used to estimate the power generated by a wind turbine.

$$P = \dfrac{D^2 \times W^3}{60}$$

where $P$ is the power generated in watts,
$D$ is the diameter of the blade in metres,
$W$ is the wind speed in mph.
Supraj says that a wind turbine with a diameter of 4 m generates more than 500 watts of power when the wind is blowing at 12 mph.
Is Supraj correct? Show your working.

**(3 marks)**

There is a lot to read here, so make sure you find the important information. You could start by writing down the values of $D$ and $W$ given in the question, then substitute into the formula.

### Top exam tip!

If a problem involves unknown letters, you might be able to solve it by forming and solving your own equation.

# 7 Sequences

## Warm up

✓ An **arithmetic** sequence has a constant difference between terms. It can increase or decrease, and could include **negative numbers**.

✓ If the common difference in an arithmetic sequence is $a$, then the $n$th term is in the form $an + c$.

$$\overset{-3}{\phantom{x}}\quad \overset{+3}{\phantom{x}}\quad \overset{+3}{\phantom{x}}\quad \overset{+3}{\phantom{x}}\quad \overset{+3}{\phantom{x}}$$
$$-11 \quad -8 \quad -5 \quad -2 \quad 1 \quad 4 \quad \ldots$$

$n$th term = $3n - 11$

$$\overset{+10}{\phantom{x}}\quad \overset{-10}{\phantom{x}}\quad \overset{-10}{\phantom{x}}\quad \overset{-10}{\phantom{x}}\quad \overset{-10}{\phantom{x}}$$
$$100 \quad 90 \quad 80 \quad 70 \quad 60 \quad 50 \quad \ldots$$

$n$th term = $-10n + 100$

✓ In a **quadratic sequence**, the **second differences** are constant. If the $n$th term is $an^2 + bn + c$ the second difference is $2a$.

✓ A sequence where you add two consecutive terms to get the next term is called a **Fibonacci sequence**.

## Reps

**1** Find the next two terms in each sequence.

|   | 2 | 5 | 8 | 11 | 14 | 17 | 20 |
|---|---|---|---|----|----|----|----|
| a | −1 | 4 | 9 | 14 | 19 | …… | …… |
| b | 15 | 11 | 7 | 3 | −1 | …… | …… |
| c | 1 | 2 | 3 | 5 | 8 | …… | …… |
| d | 1 | 2 | 4 | 7 | 11 | …… | …… |

**2** Write the first three terms in the sequences with these $n$th terms.

|   | $6n - 5$ | 1 | 7 | 13 |
|---|----------|---|---|----|
| a | $3n + 10$ | …… | …… | …… |
| b | $20 - 2n$ | …… | …… | …… |
| c | $2n^2 - 5$ | …… | …… | …… |
| d | $3n^2 - n + 1$ | …… | …… | …… |

**3** Find the $n$th term of each arithmetic sequence.

|   | 7 | 5 | 3 | 1 | −1 | $-2n + 9$ |
|---|---|---|---|---|----|-----------|
| a | 10 | 15 | 20 | 25 | 30 | ………… |
| b | −1 | 5 | 11 | 17 | 23 | ………… |
| c | 13 | 7 | 1 | −5 | −11 | ………… |
| d | 1 | 10 | 19 | 28 | 37 | ………… |

**4** Fill in the differences and second differences in this quadratic sequence, then work out the $n$th term.

$$5 \qquad 9 \qquad 15 \qquad 23 \qquad 33$$

First    +4    +…..    +…..    +……

Second    + …..    + …..    + …..

$n$th term = ……………………

## Exam practice

Links to:
Pages 22–24

**1.** The $n$th term in a sequence is $6n - 1$
Is 103 a term in this sequence?
Show how you get your answer. **(2 marks)**

> For every term in the sequence, $n$ must be a **whole number**.

**2.** The rule to get from one term to the next term in a sequence is

| Add $k$ then multiply by 2 |
|---|

The third term is 52 and the fourth term is 112
Find the first term in the sequence.
**(5 marks)**

### Problem solved!

You need to start by finding the value of $k$. Use the terms you have been given, then work backwards to find the first term.

This is a quadratic sequence. The second difference is $+6$, so the coefficient of $n^2$ will be half this number. Use the difference between $3n^2$ and each term of the sequence to work out what you need to add or subtract from $3n^2$.

**3.** Here are the first five terms of a sequence.

$$4 \qquad 14 \qquad 30 \qquad 52 \qquad 80$$

**Guided**

$$+ 10 \quad + 16 \quad + 22 \quad + 28$$
$$+ 6 \qquad + 6 \qquad + 6$$

Find an expression, in terms of $n$, for the
$n$th term of this sequence. **(3 marks)**

| $n$ | 1 | 2 | 3 | ...... | ...... |
|---|---|---|---|---|---|
| $u_n$ | 4 | 14 | ...... | ...... | ...... |
| $3n^2$ | 3 | 12 | ...... | ...... | ...... |
| $u_n - 3n^2$ | 1 | 2 | ...... | ...... | ...... |

$n$th term $= 3n^2 + $ ..............................

$n$th term $= $ ....................

### Top exam tip!

Don't assume a sequence is arithmetic until you have checked for constant differences.

## 8 ▶ Straight-line graphs

### Warm up

✓ The equation of a straight line is $y = mx + c$. The **gradient** is $m$ and the $y$-intercept is $c$.

✓ To find the equation of a straight line through two points, work out the gradient, $m$, substitute one pair of $(x, y)$ values into $y = mx + c$ and solve to find $c$.

✓ **Parallel** lines have the same gradient.

✓ If a line has gradient $m$, a **perpendicular** line will have gradient $-\dfrac{1}{m}$.

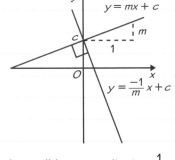

### Reps

**1** Write down the gradient and $y$-intercept of each line.

| Equation | Gradient | $y$-int |
|---|---|---|
| $y = 6x - 2$ | 6 | (0, −2) |
| **a** $y = -2x + 5$ | ...... | ......... |
| **b** $y = \frac{1}{2}x - 3$ | ...... | ......... |
| **c** $y = 11 - x$ | ...... | ......... |
| **d** $3x + y = 4$ | ...... | ......... |

**2** Find the equation of the line through each pair of points.

| Points | Equation |
|---|---|
| (0, 4) and (3, 1) | $y = -x + 4$ |
| **a** (0, 1) and (2, 5) | ............... |
| **b** (0, 10) and (4, −2) | ............... |
| **c** (3, 5) and (7, 3) | ............... |
| **d** (−2, 0) and (1, 12) | ............... |

**3** Find the equation of the line that is parallel to $y = 3x - 1$ and passes through the given point.

| Point | Equation |
|---|---|
| (0, 7) | $y = 3x + 7$ |
| **a** (0, −2) | ............... |
| **b** (0, 0) | ............... |
| **c** (1, 5) | ............... |
| **d** (−2, −2) | ............... |

**4** Match up the pairs of perpendicular lines.

$y = 2x + 8$            $y = 5 - 3x$

$y = x - 5$            $y = -\frac{1}{2}x - 1$

$4y + x = 5$            $4y = 10 - 6x$

$y = \frac{1}{3}x + 7$            $y = -x$

$3y - 2x = 5$            $y = 4x - 1$

## Exam practice

Pearson
Mathematics
Higher tier
Revision Guide

**Links to:**
Pages 25–27

**1.** Lines **A** and **B** are parallel. The points $(-8, 6)$ and $(10, q)$ are on line **A**.
Line **B** cuts the $y$-axis at $(0, q)$.

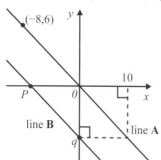

Find the coordinates of the point $P$ where line **B** crosses the $x$-axis. **(4 marks)**

Straight lines that pass through the origin have equation $y = mx$.

Draw a triangle to work out the gradient.

Lines that slope down have a negative gradient.

Gradient of line **A** $= \dfrac{-6}{8} =$ ...............

Equation of line **A:** $y =$ ........................$x$

Equation of line **B:** $y =$ ........................

$$P = (\ldots\ldots\ldots, \ldots\ldots\ldots)$$

Give both coordinates of $P$ in your answer.

## Problem solved!

Draw a sketch of the three points to work out roughly where point $R$ should be.

**2.** The points $P(1, 3)$, $Q(10, 0)$ and $R(3, k)$ form the vertices of a right-angled triangle. $QPR$ is the right angle.

Find an equation of the straight line that passes through $R$ and $Q$. **(5 marks)**

If $QPR$ is a right angle then the line segments $QP$ and $PR$ will be perpendicular.

## Top exam tip!

If you know one coordinate of a point on a line you can substitute it into the equation of the line to find the other coordinate.

......................

# 9 ▶ Quadratic equations

## Warm up

✓ Whatever method you use to solve a **quadratic equation**, you need to start by rearranging it into the form $ax^2 + bx + c = 0$.

✓ If you can **factorise** the left-hand side you can set each factor equal to zero to find the solutions.

✓ You can use the **quadratic formula**. You need to learn this:

The ± means that there can be two separate solutions.

$$x = \frac{-b \pm \sqrt{b^2 - 4ac}}{2a}$$

✓ You can **complete the square** for a quadratic expression:

$x^2 + 6x + 4 = 0$

$(x + 3)^2 - 3^2 + 4 = 0$

$(x + 3)^2 - 5 = 0$

The left-hand side is in **completed square form**. You can solve the equation using inverse operations.

$$x = -3 \pm\sqrt{5}$$

## Reps

**1** Write down the answers to each factorised quadratic equation.

$(x + 1)(x - 5) = 0 \quad x = -1 \text{ or } 5$

a $(x - 4)(x - 3) = 0 \quad x = \ldots.. \text{ or } \ldots..$

b $(x + 2)(x + 2) = 0 \quad x = \ldots..$

c $(2x + 1)(x - 7) = 0 \, x = \ldots.. \text{ or } \ldots..$

d $(x + 4)(3x - 2) = 0 \, x = \ldots.. \text{ or } \ldots..$

**2** Find the missing numbers to complete the square.

$x^2 - 4x + 1 = (x - 2)^2 - 3$

a $x^2 + 6x + 2 = (x + \ldots..)^2 - 7$

b $x^2 - 8x - 5 = (x - 4)^2 - \ldots\ldots..$

c $x^2 + 2x - 1 = (x + 1)^2 - \ldots\ldots..$

d $x^2 - 10x + 10 = (x - \ldots..)^2 - \ldots..$

**3** Rearrange into the form $ax^2 + bx + c$.

$x^2 = 4x - 1 \qquad x^2 - 4x + 1 = 0$

a $x^2 = 2 - 6x \qquad \ldots\ldots\ldots\ldots\ldots$

b $5x = 2x^2 + 1 \qquad \ldots\ldots\ldots\ldots\ldots$

c $x + 1 = 2x^2 - 2 \qquad \ldots\ldots\ldots\ldots\ldots$

d $x(x + 5) = 3x^2 \qquad \ldots\ldots\ldots\ldots\ldots$

**4** Use the quadratic formula to solve, correct to 1 decimal place.

$x^2 + 3x - 1 = 0 \quad x = -3.3 \text{ or } 0.3$

a $x^2 - 6x + 2 = 0 \quad x = \ldots... \text{ or } \ldots...$

b $2x^2 + 10x + 1 = 0 \, x = \ldots... \text{ or } \ldots...$

c $3x^2 - 6x + 2 = 0 \quad x = \ldots... \text{ or } \ldots...$

d $x^2 - x - 7 = 0 \qquad x = \ldots... \text{ or } \ldots...$

## Exam practice

Links to:
Pages 31–33

 **1.** Solve $x^2 - 8x - 1 = 0$

Write your answer in the form $a \pm \sqrt{b}$, where $a$ and $b$ are integers. **(3 marks)**

> This is a non-calculator question, so you need to solve it by **completing the square.**

$$x = \text{.........................}$$

> ## Problem solved!
>
> You can solve this problem by forming your own quadratic equation. Remember to rearrange it into the form $ax^2 + bx + c = 0$ before attempting to solve it.

**2.** The diagram shows two right-angled triangles.

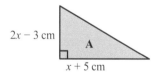

2x − 3 cm  A  x + 5 cm  B  x cm  3 cm

The ratio of the area of triangle **A** to the area of triangle **B** is $2 : 1$

Find the value of $x$. **(5 marks)**

> Your quadratic equation will have two solutions, but only one of them can represent a length. Make sure you choose the right one.

**Guided**

Area of **A** $= 2 \times$ area of **B**

$$\frac{1}{2}(2x - 3)(\text{..........}) = 2 \times \frac{1}{2}(\text{......})$$

$$\frac{1}{2}(2x^2 - 3x + \text{....}x - \text{....}) = \text{....}x$$

$$2x^2 + \text{....}x - \text{...} = \text{....}x$$

$$2x^2 \text{..........................} = 0$$

$$(2x \text{..........})(\text{..............}) = 0$$

$$x = \text{........ or ........}$$

$$x = \text{.........................}$$

> ## Top exam tip!
>
> If you are asked to give solutions to a quadratic equation to a particular degree of accuracy (such as 2 decimal places) then that is a clue that you need to use the **quadratic formula.**

# 10 Curvy graphs

## Warm up

✓ The quadratic graph $y = (x + p)^2 + q$ has a turning point at $(-p, q)$.

✓ The **roots** of $f(x) = 0$ are the points where the graph of $y = f(x)$ crosses the $x$-axis. The $x$-coordinate of the turning point is halfway between these roots.

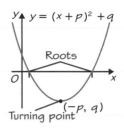

✓ Here are three other types of graph you need to be able to recognise:

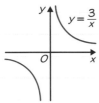

$y = \frac{k}{x}$ is a

**reciprocal** graph.

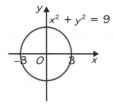

A **cubic graph** has an $x^3$ term in its equation.

The circle with centre the origin and radius $r$ has equation $x^2 + y^2 = r^2$.

## Reps

1. For each quadratic graph, find the coordinates of the turning point.

$y = (x - 3)^2 + 5$     $(3, 5)$

**a** $y = (x + 1)^2 - 6$    (...., ....)     **b** $y = x^2 + 4$          (...., ....)

**c** $y = (x - 10)^2$      (...., ....)     **d** $y = x^2 - 2x + 3$     (...., ....)

2. Match each graph to the correct equation.

$y = -x^3 + 3x^2 - 2x$     $x^2 + y^2 = 6$     $y = 10 - x^2$     $y = x^3 + x^2$

 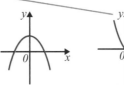 

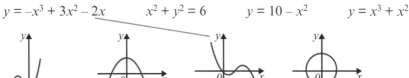

## Exam practice

Pearson
Pearson Edexcel GCSE (9-1)
**Mathematics**
Higher tier
Revision Guide
FREE

Links to:
Pages 28,
42–44

 **1. (a)** On the grid draw the graph of
$y = x^2 + 2x - 1$
You can use the table of values to help you.

**Guided**

| $x$ | $-3$ | $-2$ | $-1$ | $0$ | $1$ |
|-----|------|------|------|-----|-----|
| $y$ | 2 | $-1$ | | | |

It's sometimes easier
to draw a curve if you
turn the paper and
place your hand **inside**
the curve.

(grid with plotted points)

**(3 marks)**

The solutions are the
x-coordinates of the
points where the curve
crosses the line $y = 1$

**(b)** Write down the coordinates of the
turning point of the graph. **(1 mark)**

(................, ................)

**(c)** Write down the solutions to $x^2 + 2x - 1 = 1$
**(2 marks)**

..........................

**Problem solved!**

A **tangent** just
touches the circle at
that point. It will be
**perpendicular** to the
radius at the given
point. Start by finding
the gradient of the
line joining $(0, 0)$ to
$(4, 2)$, then find the
perpendicular gradient.

 **2.** Find the equation of the tangent to the
circle $x^2 + y^2 = 20$ at the point $(4, 2)$.
**(3 marks)**

..........................

**Top exam tip!**

Graphs of curves
should always be
drawn with a **sharp
pencil** in a **single,
smooth** curve.

# 11 ▸ Simultaneous equations

## Warm up

✓ Simultaneous equations can be solved by **elimination** or **substitution**. You need to find values of $x$ and $y$ that make **both equations true** at the same time.

✓ To solve one linear and one **quadratic** simultaneous equation, you need to use **substitution**. Write the linear equation as $x = ...$ or $y = ...$, then substitute into the quadratic equation.

✓ Solutions to simultaneous equations can represent points of intersection of graphs:

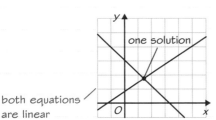

one solution

both equations are linear

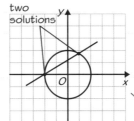

two solutions

one linear and one quadratic

## Reps

**1** Multiply every term in each linear equation by 2

$2y + 3x = 1$    $4y + 6x = 2$

**a** $x - 4y = 2$    .....................

**b** $3x + 5y = 7$    .....................

**c** $2x = 6y + 1$    .....................

**d** $y = 3 - x$    .....................

**2** Substitute $y = 3x + 1$ into each expression and simplify.

$x^2 + y - 5$    $x^2 + 3x - 4$

**a** $5x - y$    .....................

**b** $x - 3y + 1$    .....................

**c** $x^2 + y^2$    .....................

**d** $xy - 2x + 7$    .....................

**3** Solve each pair of simultaneous equations.

$x + y = 5$    **a** $2x - y = 1$    **b** $y = 2 - x$      **c** $4x - 3y = 5$

$2x - 3y = 15$      $3x + 2y = 19$      $y^2 = x + 4$      $2x + 5y = 9$

$x = 6$      $x = .......$      $x = .......$    $x = .......$      $x = .......$

$y = -1$      $y = .......$      $y = .......$    $y = .......$      $y = .......$

## Exam practice

Links to:
Pages 34–35

**1.** Solve the simultaneous equations

$x + y = 6$

$2x - 4y = 3$ **(3 marks)**

Number the simultaneous equations ① and ②. Then look for the easiest way to make one pair of coefficients equal. If you multiply equation ① by 2 you will get $2x + 2y = 12$

You can then subtract equation ② to eliminate $x$

$x = $ ........................

$y = $ ........................

### Problem solved!

**2.** A circle has the equation $x^2 + y^2 = 16$ ①

A straight line has the equation

$y - 2x = 8$ ②

Find the coordinates of the points where the circle and the line intersect.

**(6 marks)**

Solve the equation of the line and the equation of the circle simultaneously to find the coordinates of the point of intersection.

**Guided**

Rearrange ②: $y = $ ........................ ③

Substitute ③ into ①:

$x^2 + ($ ..............$)^2 = 16$

$x^2 + $ .........$x^2 + $ .........$x + $ ......... $= 16$

.........$x^2 + $ .........$x + $ ......... $= 0$

($.........$)($.........$) $= 0$

$x = $ ....... or ....... 

When $x = $ ......., $y = $ ...............................

When $x = $ ......., $y = $ ...............................

( ......., ....... ) and ( ......., ....... )

Look for ways to make your working easier. The coefficient of $y$ in the second equation is 1, so it will be easier to rearrange for $y$ and then substitute.

### Top exam tip!

Answers to simultaneous equations are **pairs** of values.

## 12 ▸ Inequalities

**12**

### Warm up

✓ When solving a linear inequality, if you multiply or divide by a **negative number** you have to **reverse** the inequality sign.

✓ You can show solutions to inequalities on number lines.

$$-1 \leqslant x < 3$$

```
 -2 -1  0  1  2  3
```

Use an open circle for $<$ and $>$ and use a closed circle for $\leqslant$ and $\geqslant$

✓ You can show linear inequalities as regions on graphs.

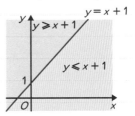

✓ Solutions to **quadratic inequalities** can have more than one part. The solutions to $x^2 - 5x > 0$ are the $x$-values where the curve is **above** the $x$-axis. So the solution is $x < 0$ **or** $x > 5$.

### Reps

**1** Write down all the integers that satisfy each inequality.

$-2 < x \leqslant 1$ \qquad $-1, 0, 1$

a $3 < x < 7$ ........................

b $-5 \leqslant x < -3$ ........................

c $0 \leqslant x \leqslant 3$ ........................

d $10 < x < 15$ ........................

**2** Solve each inequality.

$3x < x - 4$ \qquad $x < -2$

a $x + 1 \geqslant 2x + 5$ ........................

b $3x - 2 \leqslant 10$ ........................

c $5 - x > 8 - 2x$ ........................

d $x^2 - 1 < 0$ ........................

**3** Write down the inequality represented by each shaded region.

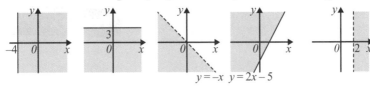

$y = -x$ \qquad $y = 2x - 5$

$x \geqslant -4$ \qquad a .......... \qquad b .......... \qquad c .......... \qquad d ..........

## Exam practice

Links to:
Pages 37,
38, 41

**1.** On the grid, shade the region that satisfies all of these inequalities.

$y \leqslant 3$ $\qquad$ $y > 1 - x$ $\qquad$ $y \geqslant 2x - 4$

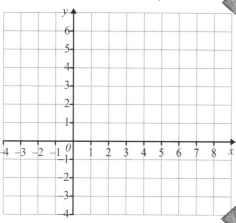

Use solid lines to represent $\leqslant$ or $\geqslant$. Use dotted lines to represent $<$ or $>$.

Label the region **R**. **(4 marks)**

Replace each inequality with $=$ to work out where the lines should be drawn. Label each line with the equation. Then shade **above** the line for $y >$ or $y \geqslant$, and **below** the line for $y <$ or $y \leqslant$.

**2.** Solve the inequality $x^2 - 1 > 2(x + 1)$.

**(4 marks)**

### Problem solved!

 **Guided**

$x^2 - 1 > 2x + 2$

$x^2 - \ldots\ldots x - \ldots\ldots > 0$

$(x\ldots\ldots)(x\ldots\ldots) > 0$

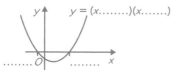

$y = (x\ldots\ldots)(x\ldots\ldots)$

So the solution is $\ldots\ldots\ldots\ldots\ldots\ldots$

Rearrange the inequality into the form:

$ax^2 + bx + c > 0$

Then **factorise** the left-hand side to work out the **critical values**. Draw a sketch to help you choose the correct set of values of x.

## Top exam tip!

Make sure the **type** of inequality in your answer matches the type used in the question.

# 13 Applications of algebra

## Warm up

✓ To **prove** an algebraic statement you need to show that it is true for **all** numbers. You can use these rules for odd and even integers in some algebra proofs.

| | Product | Sum |
|---|---|---|
| Odd and Odd | Odd | Even |
| Odd and Even | Even | Odd |
| Even and Even | Even | Even |

✓ $b^2 - 4ac$ is called the **discriminant** of the quadratic expression $ax^2 + bx + c$. You can use it to work out the number of solutions to the quadratic equation $ax^2 + bx + c = 0$

**1** $b^2 - 4ac > 0$
Two distinct solutions

**2** $b^2 - 4ac = 0$
One solution

**3** $b^2 - 4ac < 0$
No real solutions

✓ When $b^2 - 4ac = 0$ there is exactly one solution. You can use this fact to show that a line is a **tangent** to a quadratic curve or to a circle.

## Reps

**1** Assuming $k$ is an integer, write odd or even for each expression.

$2k + 1$       odd

**a** $10k$       .............

**b** $k(k + 1)$       .............

**c** $4k + 5$       .............

**d** $k + (k + 3)$       .............

**2** Work out the discriminant of each quadratic expression.

$2x^2 + 3x - 1$       17

**a** $x^2 + 2x + 1$       .............

**b** $x^2 - 5x + 3$       .............

**c** $3x^2 - x - 5$       .............

**d** $2x^2 - 1$       .............

**3** Match each $y = ax^2 + bx + c$ curve to the correct discriminant.

$b^2 - 4ac = 0$       $b^2 - 4ac > 0$       $b^2 - 4ac = 0$       $b^2 - 4ac < 0$

**GCSE Maths: Bootcamp**

## Exam practice

**Links to:**
Pages 32, 36, 52

**1.** $n$ is an integer.
Prove algebraically that
$$\frac{1}{2}(2n-1)^2 + \frac{1}{2}(2n+1)^2$$
is always an odd number. **(2 marks)**

> Expand both sets of brackets and simplify the expression. If you can show that the expression is an **odd** number plus an **even** number then you know it must be odd.

### Problem solved!

> If the line is a tangent to the circle that means it will intersect it **exactly once**. You can attempt to solve these equations simultaneously then set the discriminant equal to 0 and solve to find $k$.

**2.** The straight line with equation $y = 6 - x$ is a tangent to the circle with equation $x^2 + y^2 = k$.

Find the value of $k$. **(5 marks)**

**Guided**

$y = 6 - x$   ①

$x^2 + y^2 = k$   ②

Substitute ① into ②:

$$x^2 + (\text{...............})^2 = k$$
$$x^2 + \text{........} - \text{........} x + x^2 = k$$
$$\text{........} x^2 - \text{........} x + \text{........} - k = 0$$

Discriminant: $b^2 - 4ac = 0$

$$(\text{........})^2 - 4 \times \text{........} \times (\text{........} - k) = 0$$
$$\text{........} - \text{........} + 8k = 0$$
$$8k = \text{..........}$$
$$k = \text{........}$$

$$k = \text{.....................}$$

### Top exam tip!

If you have to **prove** something, finish with a conclusion stating what you have proved.

# Functions

## Warm up

☑ If you apply one function after another you get a **composite function**.

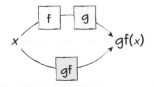

☑ The function that is the reverse of another function is called its **inverse**.

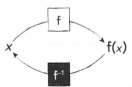

☑ You can use functions to describe a **translation** or a **reflection** of a graph. If you start with the graph $y = f(x)$:

**1** $y = f(x) + a$ is a translation by $a$ units up.

**2** $y = f(x + a)$ is a translation by $a$ units to the left.

**3** $y = -f(x)$ is a reflection in the $x$-axis.

**4** $y = f(-x)$ is a reflection in the $y$-axis.

If $a$ is negative the directions are the opposite – down or right.

## Reps

**1** $f(x) = x^2$ and $g(x) = 1 - 4x$

Evaluate

$f(4)$         16

**a** $f(-2)$   .......................

**b** $g(-3)$   .......................

**c** $g(2)$   .......................

**d** $fg(2)$   .......................

**2** $f(x) = 2x + 1$

Write down an expression for

$f(3x)$       $6x + 1$

**a** $f(x + 2)$   .......................

**b** $f(x^2)$   .......................

**c** $ff(x)$   .......................

**d** $f^{-1}(x)$   .......................

**3** Sketch the transformation shown.

$y = f(x) - 2$    **a** $y = f(x + 3)$   **b** $y = -f(x)$   **c** $y = f(-x)$

Pearson
Revise

Pearson Edexcel GCSE (9-1)
**Mathematics**
Higher tier
Revision Guide

FREE

## Exam practice

**Links to:**
Pages 40,
50–51

**1.** The functions f and g are such that

$f(x) = 2(x - 5)$ and $g(x) = \frac{x}{3} - 1$

**(a)** Find the value of g(30)  **(1 mark)**

$g(30) = \dots\dots\dots\dots\dots$

**(b)** Find $f^{-1}(x)$  **(2 marks)**

$y = 2(x - 5)$

$y = \dots\dots x - \dots\dots$

$y + \dots\dots = \dots\dots x$

$\dfrac{y + \dots\dots}{\dots\dots} = x$

$f^{-1}(x) = \dots\dots\dots\dots\dots$

**(c)** Find ff(x)  **(2 marks)**

$ff(x) = f(\dots\dots\dots)$

$= 2(\dots\dots\dots - 5)$

$= \dots\dots\dots\dots\dots$

$ff(x) = \dots\dots\dots\dots\dots$

**2.** The grid shows the graph with equation $y = f(x)$.

On the same grid, sketch the graph with equation $y = -f(x + 2)$.  **(2 marks)**

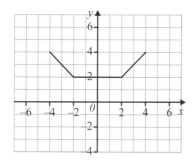

---

Follow these steps to find the inverse of a function:

1. **Write** the original function as $y = \dots\dots$

2. **Rearrange** to make x the subject.

3. **Swap** y for x on the right-hand side and write the answer as $f^{-1}(x) = \dots\dots$

ff(x) is the composite function formed by applying f twice.

### Problem solved!

There are **two** transformations to consider here. Start with $y = f(x + 2)$ then apply the transformation for $y = -f(x)$.

### Top exam tip!

Use brackets when substituting a value or expression into a function.

# 15 ▷ Gradient and area

**Reps**

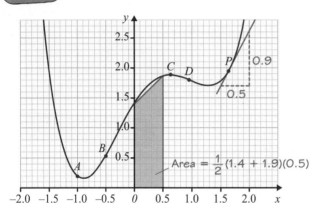

$$\text{Area} = \frac{1}{2}(1.4 + 1.9)(0.5)$$

**1** Estimate the gradient of the curve at each point.

| | | |
|---|---|---|
| $P$ | | 1.8 |
| **a** $A$ | | .................. |
| **b** $B$ | | .................. |
| **c** $C$ | | .................. |
| **d** $D$ | | .................. |

**2** Use strips 0.5 wide to estimate the area under the curve between

| | | |
|---|---|---|
| 0 and 0.5 | | 0.825 |
| **a** 0.5 and 1 | | .................. |
| **b** 1.5 and 1 | | .................. |
| **c** –1 and 0 | | .................. |
| **d** –1 and 1 | | .................. |

**Exam practice**

**Links to:**
Pages 54–56

**1.** A robotic vacuum cleaner travels down a hallway. It moves at 0.1 m/s for the first 2 minutes. It then stops at a charging station for 1 minute, before returning in 4 minutes. Draw a travel graph for this journey.

**(3 marks)**

Watch out! The speed of the vacuum cleaner is given in **metres per second**, but the scale on the graph is in minutes.

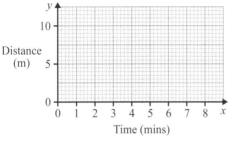

Time (mins)

Draw three strips of width 5 seconds and work out the area of each strip. The area of this trapezium is given by:

$$\frac{1}{2}h(a + b)$$

**2.** Here is a speed–time graph for a car.

**Guided**

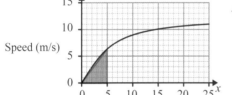

Speed (m/s)

Time (s)

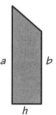

**(a)** Work out an estimate for the distance travelled by the car in the first 15 seconds. **(3 marks)**

For part (b), Look at whether the trapeziums are above or below the curve.

$$\frac{1}{2}(5 \times 6.5) + \text{............} + \text{............}$$

= .......

.........................m

**(b)** Is your answer an overestimate or an underestimate? Give a reason for your answer. **(1 mark)**

**Top exam tip!**

Always use a ruler and a sharp pencil when you are drawing on graphs in your exam. A transparent ruler makes it easier to draw accurately.

# 16 Ratio and proportion

## Warm up

☑ To divide a number in a given ratio:

| Work out the total number of parts in the ratio | ⇒ | Divide the amount by the total parts to find the value of one part | ⇒ | Multiply the value of one part by each part in the ratio to find the amounts | ⇒ | Check the amounts add to the correct total |

☑ If two quantities are in **direct proportion** when one doubles, the other doubles.

$y \propto x$

☑ If two quantities are in **inverse proportion** when one doubles, the other halves.

$y \propto \dfrac{1}{x}$

☑ Solve proportion problems by writing a formula. For example, if $y$ is inversely proportional to $x^2$, write $y = \dfrac{k}{x^2}$ then solve to find $k$.

## Reps

**1** Write these ratios in simplest form.

12:18          2:3

a 5:10          ......................

b 25:10          ......................

c 12:30:15          ......................

**2** Divide £600 in the following ratios.

2:1          £400 and £200

a 1:3          £....... and £.......

b 5:1          £....... and £.......

c 1:9          £....... and £.......

**3** $y$ is directly proportional to $x$.
When $y = 3$, $x = 10$
Find

$y$ when $x = 20$          6

a $y$ when $x = 5$          ......................

b $x$ when $y = 15$          ......................

c $y$ when $x = 8$          ......................

**4** 12 kg of potatoes cost £9.12
Find the cost of the following amounts.

3 kg          £2.28

a 1 kg          ......................

b 5 kg          ......................

c 750 g          ......................

## Exam practice

1. A bag contains solid balls and hollow balls. They are all either red or white.

   - The ratio of red to white balls is $2:1$

   - The ratio of the number of solid red balls to the number of hollow red balls is $9:11$

   - The ratio of the number of solid white balls to the number of hollow white balls is $3:7$

   Work out what fraction of all the balls are solid. **(4 marks)**

**Links to:**
Pages 60, 61, 68–70

**Problem solved!**

You can solve some ratio problems by converting to fractions.

If the ratio of red to white balls is $2:1$, then $\frac{2}{3}$ of the balls are red and $\frac{1}{3}$ are white.

..........................

Write a formula using $k$ for the **constant of proportionality**. Then use the numbers given in the question to find the value of $k$.

2. $y$ is directly proportional to $x^2$
   $y = 1600$ when $x = 20$
   Find the value of $y$ when $x = 25$  **(3 marks)**

   **Guided**

   $y = kx^2$

   $1600 = k \times 20^2$

   $k = \ldots \div \ldots = \ldots$

   $y = \ldots x^2$

   $= \ldots \times \ldots^2$

   $= \ldots$

   $y = \ldots\ldots\ldots\ldots\ldots$

**Top exam tip!**

If you need to compare two things to decide which one is better value, work out what **one** unit of each one would cost. For example, the cost per gram of cereal in two different-sized boxes.

# 17 Compound measures

## Warm up

✓ To convert metric units multiply or divide by 10, 100 or 1000:

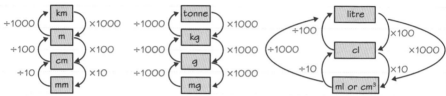

✓ Learn the formula triangles for **speed** and **density**.

$$\text{speed} = \frac{\text{distance}}{\text{time}}$$

$$\text{density} = \frac{\text{mass}}{\text{volume}}$$

✓ To convert units of area use a length multiplier **squared**.

✓ To convert units of volume use a length multiplier **cubed**.

## Reps

**1** Convert

0.2 m into cm     20   cm

**a** 65 cm into m    ............... m

**b** 0.15 litres into ml   ............... ml

**c** 2400 g into kg    ............... kg

**d** 420 m into km    ............... km

**3** Complete the missing values in the table.

| | Mass (g) | Volume (cm³) | Density (g/cm³) |
|---|---|---|---|
| | 12 | 1.5 | 8 |
| **a** | 100 | 8 | ....... |
| **b** | 660 | ....... | 2.2 |
| **c** | ....... | 250 | 1.6 |

**2** A cyclist travels 30 km. Work out her average speed if she takes

2 hours    15   km/h

**a** 6 hours    ............... km/h

**b** 2.5 hours    ............... km/h

**c** 90 minutes    ............... km/h

**d** $1\frac{1}{4}$ hours    ............... km/h

**4** Convert

2 cm² into mm²    200   mm²

**a** 0.8 m² into cm²    ............... cm²

**b** 300 mm³ into cm³    ............... cm³

**c** 0.025 km² into m²    ............... m²

**d** 0.004 m³ into cm³    ............... cm³

## Exam practice

**Links to:**
Pages
65–67, 81

 **1.** An iron block has a mass of 22.8 kg.
The density of iron is 7.9 g/cm³.
Work out the volume of the block.
Give your answer correct to
3 significant figures.

**(3 marks)**

> Watch out. The mass of the block is given in kilograms, but the units of density are **grams** per cm³. Convert kilograms to grams before calculating.

........................ cm³

> Make sure you round your answer to 3 s.f.

 **2.** Two friends drove at constant speeds on the M8 from Glasgow to Edinburgh. Hamid took $1\frac{1}{2}$ hours to complete the 75 km journey. Chloe started her journey 15 minutes after Hamid, and caught up with him 45 minutes later.
Work out Chloe's speed. **(5 marks)**

> If you are entering mixed numbers on your calculator, use your calculator to convert them to decimals first.
> $1\frac{1}{2} = 1.5$

**Guided** Hamid's speed:

$$\frac{D}{T} = \frac{............}{............} = ....... \text{ km/h}$$

After 1 hour he had travelled ....... km

Chloe's speed = $\frac{............}{............}$ = .......

........................ km/h

## Problem solved!

> If you can't see a complete strategy for the question, think about what you **can** work out easily. You know Hamid's time and distance, so you can calculate his speed.

## Top exam tip!

Make sure your units are consistent before you use the formulae for speed or density.

# 18 Growth and decay

## Warm up

✓ Growth and decay problems involve **repeated percentage change**. Use this formula to solve growth and decay problems:

Amount after *n* steps = Starting amount × Multiplier$^n$

✓ **Compound interest** means the interest earned is added to the balance before the next round of interest is calculated.

✓ **Exponential graphs** show growth and decay.

The graph of $y = a^x$ always passes through (0, 1). If $a > 1$ then the graph slopes up (growth) and if $0 < a < 1$ then the graph slopes down (decay)

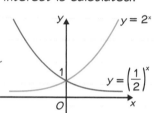

## Reps

**1** If $P = 200 \times 0.8^n$, find $P$ when

$n = 2$              128

a $n = 1$     ........................

b $n = 3$     ........................

c $n = 0$     ........................

d $n = 5$     ........................

**2** Complete this table showing 5% per annum compound interest.

| Initial amount | £2000 |
|---|---|
| End of year 1 | £2100 |
| End of year 2 | £.................. |
| End of year 3 | £.................. |
| End of year 4 | £.................. |

**3** Match each equation to the correct line.

$y = 2^x$    a $y = 3^x$    b $y = 2^{-x}$    c $y = 1.5^x$    d $y = \left(\frac{3}{4}\right)^x$

B    ..............    ..............    ..............    ..............

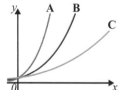

## Exam practice

**Links to:**
Pages 53, 64

**1.** Poppy and Suresh each buy a used car. Poppy's car cost £2400 and will depreciate by 10% each year. Suresh's car cost £3500 and will depreciate by 15% each year. Whose car will be worth more after 5 years? You must show all your working.

**(3 marks)**

**Depreciate** means go down in value. Because this is a repeated percentage decrease, you can use the formula for exponential growth or decay.

**Guided**

Poppy: $2400 \times 0.9^n$

Value after 5 years $= 2400 \times 0.9^{......}$

$= £...............$

Suresh: $............... \times .......^n$

Value after 5 years $= ............... \times .......$

$= £...............$

So ...............'s car will be worth more.

Use the √ key on your calculator to find the multiplier for 1 year.

**2.** Alison has invested £1800 in a savings account. The account earns $p\%$ compound interest per annum. After 4 years, her investment is worth £1986.86 Work out the value of $p$. **(3 marks)**

**Per annum** means 'each year'.

## Problem solved!

Remember $p$ is the percentage, not the multiplier.

## Top exam tip!

If a question involves growth or decay, write out the formula. You can check your formula by substituting $n = 0$.

$p = .....................$

## 19    All the angles

 Learn these angle facts:

- Alternate angles are equal ($a = b$)
- Corresponding angles are equal ($a = c$)
- Vertically opposite angles are equal ($b = c$)
- Allied angles add up to 180° ($a + d = 180°$)
- Angles around a point add up to 360° ($b + c + d + e = 360°$)
- Angles on a straight line add up to 180° ($b + d = 180°$)
- Opposite angles in a parallelogram are equal ($b = f$)

 In a regular $n$-sided polygon:

- Sum of interior angles = $180° \times (n - 2)$

- Sum of exterior angles = 360°, so each exterior angle = $\dfrac{360°}{n}$

### Reps

**1** Write in the missing angles on this diagram.

**2** Write in the missing angles on this diagram.

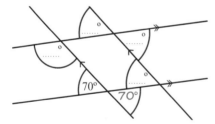

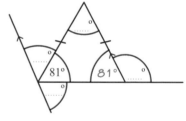

**3** Complete the missing values in the table showing angles in regular polygons.

|   | Number of sides | Interior angle | Exterior angle |
|---|---|---|---|
|   | 6 | 120° | 60° |
| a | 8 | ........° | ........° |
| b | ........ | ........° | 18° |
| c | ........ | 144° | ........° |

## Exam practice

Links to:
Pages 73–75

**1.** In the diagram, *ABFE* is a parallelogram, and *BCD* is a straight line.

 **Guided**

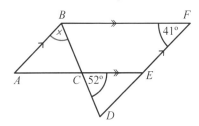

Show that angle *ABC* = 87° **(4 marks)**

Angle ACB = ....... °

Reason: ....................................................

Angle BAC = ....... °

Reason: ....................................................

So ....... ° + ....... ° + x = 180°

Reason: ....................................................

x = 180° − ....... ° = ....... °

Angles are labelled with the vertex in the middle. Angle ABC has been marked with an *x* on the diagram.

The question says 'show that.' You need to show all your working and write down the angle facts you use.

Write in angles on the diagram as you work them out.

**Problem solved!**

**2.** This pattern is made from identical regular polygons **A**, and equilateral triangles.

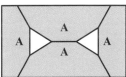

Work out the size of one **exterior** angle of **A**.

Work out the number of sides of polygon **A**. **(4 marks)**

**Top exam tip!**

When you are answering questions about **regular polygons**, it's often easier to use **exterior angles** rather than interior angles.

....................

**Workout 19** ☐

# 20 Trigonometry

## Warm up

✓ Use the SOH CAH TOA rules for **right-angled** triangles:

- $\sin x = \dfrac{opp}{hyp}$, $\cos x = \dfrac{adj}{hyp}$, $\tan x = \dfrac{opp}{adj}$

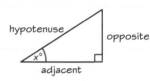

✓ The **sine rule** and the **cosine rule** work for **any** triangle:

- $\dfrac{\sin A}{a} = \dfrac{\sin B}{b} = \dfrac{\sin C}{c}$
- $a^2 = b^2 + c^2 - 2bc\cos A$

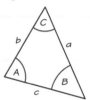

✓ You need to be able to remember the exact values of sin, cos and tan of 0°, 30°, 45°, 60° and 90° **without a calculator**.

## Reps

① Find the sizes of the missing angles to 1 decimal place.

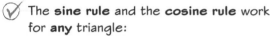

ⓐ

9 m · 39.3° · 11 m

ⓑ

19 cm · 15 cm

ⓒ

4 m · 2 m

ⓓ

4 cm · 5 cm · 85°

② Find the missing side lengths.

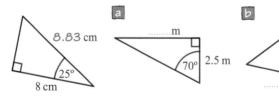

8.83 cm · 25° · 8 cm

ⓐ

........ m · 70° · 2.5 m

ⓑ

9.4 m · 40° · ........ m

ⓒ

9 m · 50° · ........ m · 8 m

## Exam practice

Links to:
Pages 77–79,
99, 100

**1.** *ADC* and *ABC* are triangles. Angle *ABC* is a right angle.

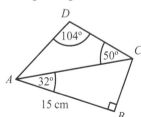

Find the length of *AD*. Give your answer correct to 1 decimal place. **(4 marks)**

ABC is a right-angled triangle so you can use the SOH CAH TOA rules.

ACD is **not** a right-angled triangle, so you will need to use either the **sine rule** or the **cosine rule**.

 ..................... cm

### Problem solved!

$\cos 0° = 1$,
$\cos 45° = \dfrac{\sqrt{2}}{2}$ and
$\cos 90° = 0$. Use this to write equations involving $a$ and $b$.

**2.** The table shows values of $x$ and $y$ that satisfy the equation $y = a + b \cos x°$.

| $x$ | 0 | 45 | 90 |
|-----|---|-----|----|
| $y$ | 5 | $3 + \sqrt{2}$ | 3 |

Find the exact value of $y$ when $x = 30$
**(4 marks)**

Once you have found $a$ and $b$ you can substitute $x = 30$ into the equation.

 Guided

$\cos 0° = $ ...... so ...... + ...... × ...... = 5

$\cos 90° = $ ......

so ...... + ...... × ...... = ......

$a = $ ...... and $b = $ ......

So $y = a + b \cos 30°$

$= $ ...... + ...... × ......

$= $ ......................

### Top exam tip!

Write out any trigonometry rules you are using before you substitute – you can sometimes get a mark just for knowing the correct rule.

**Workout 20** ☐

# 21 Length, area and volume

## Warm up

 Learn **Pythagoras' theorem** for right-angled triangles:

$$a^2 + b^2 = c^2$$

 Use this rule to find the area of **any triangle**:

$$\text{Area} = \frac{1}{2}ab\sin C$$

 A **prism** has a constant cross-section:

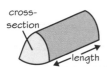

Volume = area of cross-section × length

 You need to know how to find the area of a **trapezium**:

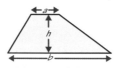

$$\text{Area} = \frac{1}{2}(a + b)h$$

## Reps

**1** Find the missing lengths in these triangles.

**a**

7.21 cm   4 cm   6 cm

5 m   8 m   ........ m

**b**

4 m   7 m   ........ m

**c**

........ cm   22 cm   16 cm

**2** Find the areas or volumes of these shapes and solids.

**a**

4 m   25°   5 m

12 cm   15 cm   20 cm

**b**

9 cm   70°   11 cm

**c**

2.0 cm   2.2 cm   4.8 cm   6.5 cm

$A = 4.23\,\text{m}^2$    $A = \text{.......}\,\text{cm}^2$    $A = \text{.......}\,\text{cm}^2$    $V = \text{.......}\,\text{cm}^3$

## Exam practice

**1.** The diagram shows a cuboid.

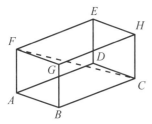

$AB = 11$ cm and $BC = 16$ cm.
The diagonal $FC = 21$ cm.
Calculate the volume of the cuboid.

**(4 marks)**

Mathematics
Higher tier
Revision Guide

**Links to:**
Pages 76,
80–82, 102

You can apply
Pythagoras' theorem in
**three dimensions**:

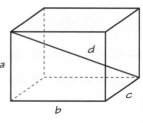

$$a^2 + b^2 + c^2 = d^2$$

 Guided

$.......^2 + .......^2 + AF^2 = .......^2$

$AF = \sqrt{\rule{3cm}{0pt}}$

$AF = .......$

Volume = ....... × ....... × ....... = .......

..........................$cm^3$

### Problem solved!

You will need to form
an equation in $x$ then
solve it. Remember
that any lengths must
be **positive numbers**.

**2.** The diagram shows a triangle.

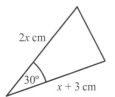

$2x$ cm

$30°$

$x + 3$ cm

The area of this triangle is 35 $cm^2$.
Find the value of $x$. **(4 marks)**

This is not a right-
angled triangle, so use

$$\text{Area} = \frac{1}{2}ab\sin C$$

### Top exam tip!

Always check that
your answers make
sense. Diagrams
are not drawn to
scale, but they will
often look **roughly** in
proportion.

$x = ..........................$ $cm^2$

# 22 ▶ Circles, sectors and cylinders

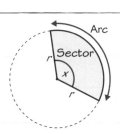

## Warm up

- ✓ A circle with radius $r$ has area $\pi r^2$ and circumference $2\pi r$

- ✓ Sector area $= \dfrac{x}{360°} \times \pi r^2$

- ✓ Arc length $= \dfrac{x}{360°} \times 2\pi r$

- ✓ You need to know the formulae for a **cylinder**:
  - Volume $= \pi r^2 h$
  - Surface area $= 2\pi rh + 2\pi r^2$

- ✓ If you need to use the formulae for the volume of a cone, sphere or pyramid in your exam they will be **given to you** with the question.

## Reps

**1** Work out the missing values for these cylinders.

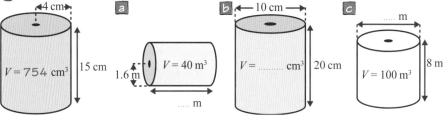

**2** Find the area of each sector and the length of the arc $AB$.

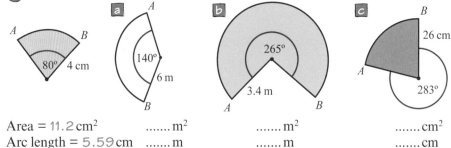

Area = 11.2 cm²     ........m²     ........m²     ........cm²
Arc length = 5.59 cm   ........m     ........m     ........cm

## Exam practice

Pearson
Revise
Pearson Edexcel GCSE (9-1)
**Mathematics**
Higher tier
Revision Guide
FREE

**Links to:**
Pages 83–86

**1.** The diagram shows a sector of a circle.

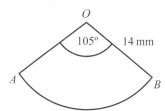

Find its perimeter. **(3 marks)**

Make sure you find the **total** distance around the shape. You need to find the length of the arc then add on two radii as well.

**Guided**

Arc length $= \dfrac{x}{360°} \times 2\pi r$

Write out the formula before you substitute.

$= \dfrac{\text{........}}{360°} \times 2\pi \times \text{.......}$

$= \text{.....................}$

Perimeter $= \text{.......} + \text{.......} + \text{.......}$

$\text{.....................}$ mm

**2.** A paperweight is made in the shape of a solid hemisphere.

Volume of sphere $= \dfrac{4}{3}\pi r^3$
Surface area of a sphere $= 4\pi r^2$

The total surface area of the hemisphere is $48\pi \, \text{cm}^2$.
Find the exact volume of the hemisphere. Give your answer in terms of $\pi$. **(4 marks)**

$\text{.....................}$ cm$^3$

### Problem solved!

Use the information given in the question to write an equation.

1. The total surface area includes the circular base of the hemisphere.

2. Write the **total** surface area in terms of $r$ and set it equal to $48\pi$.

3. Solve to find $r$.

4. Use your value of $r$ to find the volume.

### Top exam tip!

You can work out the formulae for arc length and sector area by thinking of them as fractions of a full circle.

**Workout 22**

# 23 Transformations

✓ A **translation** is a sliding movement.

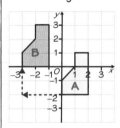

Translation of **A** → **B** by the vector $\begin{pmatrix} -3 \\ 2 \end{pmatrix}$

✓ You **reflect** a shape in a mirror line.

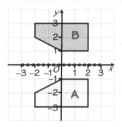

Reflection of **A** → **B** in the x-axis

✓ A **rotation** must have a centre.

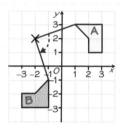

Rotation of **A** → **B** 90° clockwise about centre of rotation (–2, 2)

✓ **Enlargements** change the size of a shape. The **scale factor, k,** tells you how much bigger or smaller the shape will be.

**1** $k > 1$: shape gets **larger**

**2** $0 < k < 1$: shape gets **smaller**

**3** $k < 0$: shape is on **other side** of centre and **upside down**

## Reps

**1** On the grid, transform **T** by:

**A:** translation by vector $\begin{pmatrix} 4 \\ -3 \end{pmatrix}$

**B:** rotation 90° clockwise about $O$

**C:** enlargement centre $O$ with scale factor 2

**D:** translation by vector $\begin{pmatrix} 0 \\ 5 \end{pmatrix}$

**E:** enlargement centre $O$ with scale factor –1

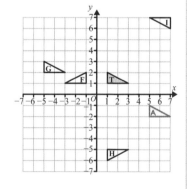

**2** Describe the transformation from **T** to:

**F:** reflection in the y-axis

**G:** ...........................................

**H:** ...........................................

**I:** ...........................................

## Exam practice

Links to:
Pages 88–90

**1.**

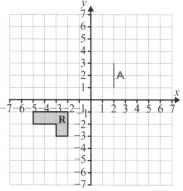

(a) Rotate shape **R** 180° about the origin. Label the new shape **A**. **(1 mark)**

(b) Translate shape **R** by the vector $\begin{pmatrix} -1 \\ 4 \end{pmatrix}$.

Label the new shape **B**. **(1 mark)**

**2.** Complete each statement:

(a) A translation by vector $\begin{pmatrix} 2 \\ 5 \end{pmatrix}$ followed

by a translation by vector $\begin{pmatrix} -3 \\ 1 \end{pmatrix}$ is

the same as a translation by vector

$\begin{pmatrix} \ldots\ldots\ldots \\ \ldots\ldots\ldots \end{pmatrix}$. **(1 mark)**

(b) An enlargement scale factor 3 with centre $O$ followed by an enlargement scale factor $\frac{1}{2}$ with centre $O$ is the same as an enlargement scale factor ....... with centre ......... .

**(1 mark)**

You can use tracing paper in your exam. Check a rotation by tracing the shape, then placing your pencil point on the centre of rotation. When you rotate the tracing paper your tracing should line up with your image.

**Problem solved!**

If you're struggling to do this in your head, try sketching a shape on some squared paper to help you.

Scale factor 3 makes the shape bigger, then scale factor $\frac{1}{2}$ makes it smaller.

**Top exam tip!**

When you rotate, reflect or translate a shape, the resulting image is **congruent** to the original shape.

Workout 23

# 24 ▸ Similar and congruent

## Reps

**1** Find the missing lengths in each pair of similar shapes.

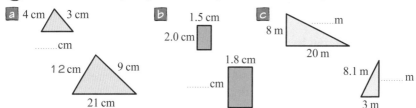

**a** 4 cm, 3 cm, ........cm, 12 cm, 9 cm, 21 cm

**b** 1.5 cm, 2.0 cm, 1.8 cm, ........cm

**c** 8 m, ........m, 20 m, 8.1 m, ........m, 3 m

**2** Write down the condition that shows that each pair of triangles is congruent.

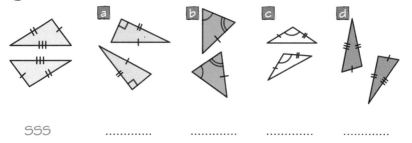

SSS ............ ............ ............ ............

## Exam practice

**Links to:**
Pages 96–98

**1.** Two cylinders **A** and **B** are mathematically similar. The ratio of the surface area of cylinder **A** to the surface area of cylinder **B** is 25 : 64

The volume of cylinder **A** is 20 cm³.
Show that the volume of cylinder **B** is 81.92 cm³. **(3 marks)**

> You are told the ratio of the surface **areas**, so use $k^2$ for the scale factor. Find the **linear scale factor**, $k$, then multiply the volume of **A** by $k^3$.

 **Guided**

$$25 \times k^2 = 64$$

$$k^2 = \ldots\ldots$$

$$k = \ldots\ldots$$

Volume of B = ....... × .......

= ............................ cm³

> Diagrams in your exam are **not drawn to scale** unless the question states that they are.

**2.** The two rectangles shown in this diagram are similar.

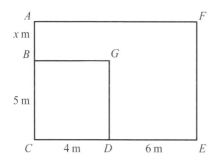

Find the **two** possible values of $x$.
**(5 marks)**

### Problem solved!

Similar shapes can be rotated. The red lines here show corresponding edges for the two possibilities:

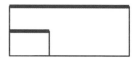

$x = \ldots\ldots\ldots$ or $x = \ldots\ldots\ldots$

## Top exam tip!

When you are comparing similar shapes, always make sure you are comparing lengths of **corresponding sides**.

## 25 Circle theorems

### Warm up

✓ A tangent to a circle makes a right angle with the radius.

✓ Tangents that meet at a point are the same length.

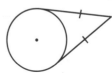

✓ Learn these three **circle theorems**:

**1** Angle at the centre of a circle is twice the angle at the circumference.

**2** Angle between a tangent and a chord is equal to the angle in the alternate segment.

**3** Opposite angles in a cyclic quadrilateral add up to 180°.

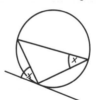

### Reps

**1** Find the missing angles in these circles with centre *O*.

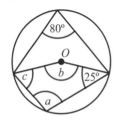

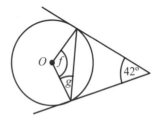

$a = 100°$ 　　 $b =$ ............° 　　 $c =$ ............° 　　 $d =$ ............°

$e =$ ............° 　　 $f =$ ............° 　　 $g =$ ............°

## Exam practice

**1.** The diagram shows a circle with centre $O$.

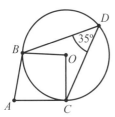

$AB$ and $AC$ are tangents to the circle, and angle $BDC = 35°$.
Find the size of angle $BAC$.
Give a reason for each stage of your working. **(4 marks)**

**Links to:**
Pages
104–105

Work out any angles you know and write them on the diagram. $AC$ and $AB$ are tangents so you know they make **right angles** with the corresponding radii.

### Problem solved!

This question doesn't **use** any of the circle theorems – it asks you to **prove** one of them. You can't use any circle theorems in your proof but you can use angle facts about straight lines and isosceles triangles.

**2.** $AC$ is a diameter of the circle with centre $O$.
$B$ is a point on the circumference of the circle.

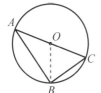

Prove that angle $ABC = 90°$.
You may **not** use any circle theorems in your proof. **(4 marks)**

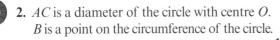

Let $\angle OBA = x$ and $\angle OBC = y$

$OB = OC$ because they are both ...........

### Top exam tip!

Remember to give reasons for each step of your working in questions involving angle facts.

**Workout 25** ☐

# 26 Vectors

## Warm up

✓ **Vectors** have a magnitude (size) and a direction.

✓ You can multiply a vector by a number called a **scalar**.

- Positive number: same direction but different magnitude.

  a
  3a

- Negative number: opposite direction.

  b
  −b

✓ Remember these two key facts for **vector proof**:

**1** If one vector is a scalar multiple of another then the vectors are **parallel**.

**2** Vectors between points that are **collinear** (lie on the same straight line) are parallel.

## Reps

**1** Use the vectors on the right to find

$$\mathbf{p} = \begin{pmatrix} 2 \\ 6 \end{pmatrix} \qquad \mathbf{q} = \begin{pmatrix} 5 \\ 1 \end{pmatrix} \qquad \mathbf{r} = \begin{pmatrix} 7 \\ 3 \end{pmatrix}$$

$$\mathbf{q} + \mathbf{r} = \begin{pmatrix} 12 \\ 4 \end{pmatrix}$$

**a** $3\mathbf{p} = \begin{pmatrix} \dots \\ \dots \end{pmatrix}$

**b** $\mathbf{q} - \mathbf{r} = \begin{pmatrix} \dots \\ \dots \end{pmatrix}$

**c** $5\mathbf{q} + 2\mathbf{p} = \begin{pmatrix} \dots \\ \dots \end{pmatrix}$

**d** $\frac{1}{2}(\mathbf{q} + \mathbf{r}) = \begin{pmatrix} \dots \\ \dots \end{pmatrix}$

**2** $P$, $R$ and $Q$ are the midpoints of $OA$, $OB$ and $AB$, respectively.

Write in terms of $\mathbf{p}$ and $\mathbf{q}$

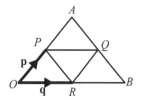

$$\overrightarrow{OA} \qquad 2\mathbf{p}$$

**a** $\overrightarrow{PQ}$ ............

**b** $\overrightarrow{BO}$ ............

**c** $\overrightarrow{AQ}$ ............

**d** $\overrightarrow{BP}$ ............

**Exam practice** ✗

1. The vectors **a** and **b** are defined as

$$\mathbf{a} = \begin{pmatrix} 10 \\ 8 \end{pmatrix} \qquad \mathbf{b} = \begin{pmatrix} 6 \\ k \end{pmatrix}$$

Given that **a** and **b** are parallel, find the value of $k$. **(2 marks)**

 **Links to:** Pages 106–107

> If two vectors are parallel then one must be a **scalar** (number) multiple of the other.

$k =$ ........................

**2**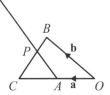

$OCB$ is a triangle.
$A$ is the midpoint of $OC$, and $P$ lies on $BC$ such that $CP : PB = 2 : 1$
$APQ$ is a straight line and $AP : PQ = 1 : 2$
$\overrightarrow{OA} = \mathbf{a}$ and $\overrightarrow{OB} = \mathbf{b}$
Prove that $QBO$ is a straight line. **(4 marks)**

> $\overrightarrow{OA}$ is another way of writing the vector from $O$ to $A$.

**Problem solved!**

> To prove that $QBO$ is a straight line you need to find the vector $\overrightarrow{OQ}$ and show that it is a multiple of **b** only. This would mean that $OB$ and $OQ$ are parallel and so $O$, $B$ and $Q$ must lie on the same straight line.

**Guided**

$\overrightarrow{OC} = $ .....**a**

$\overrightarrow{CB} = -\overrightarrow{OC} + \overrightarrow{OB} = \mathbf{b} - $ .....**a**

$\overrightarrow{CP} = \dfrac{.....}{.....}\overrightarrow{CB} = \dfrac{.....}{.....}(\mathbf{b} - $ .....**a**$)$

$\overrightarrow{AP} = \overrightarrow{AC} + \overrightarrow{CP} = $ ...............

$\overrightarrow{AQ} = $ .....$\overrightarrow{AP} = $ ...............

$\overrightarrow{OQ} = \mathbf{a} + \overrightarrow{AQ} = $ ...............

So ...............................

**Top exam tip!**

> In proof questions, always write a conclusion stating what you have proved.

# 27 Averages and range

## Warm up

✓ **Mean** = $\dfrac{\text{total of data values}}{\text{number of data values}}$

✓ **Mode** = most commonly occuring value

✓ If data is given in a **frequency table** you need to look at the frequency, f, and the data value (or midpoint), x in each row:

**Mean** = $\dfrac{\sum fx}{\sum f}$ —— This means 'the total of the $f \times x$ values divided by the sum of the frequencies'.

## Reps

**1** For each set of data values find the mean, the median and the range.

3   11   3   8   5      Mean = 6   Median = 5   Range = 8

**a** 1.4   2.0   2.1   3.5   Mean = ......   Median = ......   Range = ......

**b** 2   2   3   4   8   8   Mean = ......   Median = ......   Range = ......

**c** 2   7   8   5   5   Mean = ......   Median = ......   Range = ......

**d** 10   15   22   13   Mean = ......   Median = ......   Range = ......

**2** This frequency table shows the heights of some plants. Complete the table and find the mean and the class interval which contains the median.

| Height ($h$ cm) | Frequency ($f$) | Midpoint ($x$) | $f \times x$ |
|---|---|---|---|
| $0 \leqslant h < 10$ | 36 | 5 | 36 × 5 = 180 |
| $10 \leqslant h < 20$ | 40 | | |
| $20 \leqslant h < 30$ | 24 | | |
| Totals | | | |

Mean = ........................ cm

Class interval containing median = ........................

**Links to:**
Pages
110–112

## Exam practice

**1.** The frequency table shows the number of trips abroad taken by each member of a class in the last year.

Guided

| Number of trips | Frequency | $f \times x$ |
|---|---|---|
| 0 | 8 | $8 \times 0 = 0$ |
| 1 | 10 | |
| 2 | 7 | |
| 3 | 5 | |
| 4 | 1 | |
| Total | | |

Add a column for frequency × number of trips, and a row for the totals.

**(a)** Work out the mean number of trips. **(3 marks)**

Check that your answers make sense. Everyone in the class took between 0 and 4 trips, so the mean must be between 0 and 4

.........................

**(b)** Work out the median number of trips taken. **(2 marks)**

.........................

If you wrote the data values in order of size, the first 8 values would be 0 and the next 10 would be 1

**2.** The mean of the following five numbers is 12.6

18    7    $x$    16    $x$

Find the value of $x$. **(4 marks)**

**Problem solved!**

The total of the five values will be $5 \times 12.6$

**Top exam tip!**

Don't guess values. Trial and improvement methods are not likely to work in your exam.

$x = $ .........................

**Workout 27** ☐

# 28 Representing data

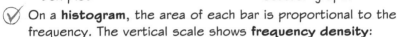

✓ You need to be able to represent and interpret data on a:
- pie chart
- cumulative frequency graph
- box plot
- histogram
- frequency polygon
- scatter graph.

✓ On a **histogram**, the area of each bar is proportional to the frequency. The vertical scale shows **frequency density**:

$$\text{Frequency density} = \frac{\text{frequency}}{\text{class width}}$$

✓ You can use a **scatter graph** or **scatter diagram** to show **correlation** and predict values using a **line of best fit**.

## Reps

① Draw a box plot to show the following information about the marks out of 30 scored by students on a test.

| Lowest score | 5 |
|---|---|
| Lower quartile | 11 |
| Median | 20 |
| Upper quartile | 25 |
| Highest score | 29 |

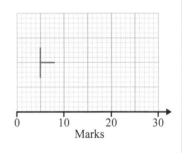

Marks

② The table shows information about the masses of eggs, from a sample of 50 eggs.

| Mass (*m* g) | Frequency | Frequency density |
|---|---|---|
| $50 \leqslant m < 60$ | 18 | 1.8 |
| $60 \leqslant m < 70$ | 25 | ............... |
| $70 \leqslant m < 80$ | 7 | ............... |

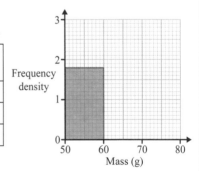

Mass (g)

a Draw a histogram for this data.

b On the same axes, draw a frequency polygon for this data.

## Exam practice

This cumulative frequency graph shows information about the heights of 120 boys in a sixth form college.

**Links to:**
Pages 113–114, 118–121

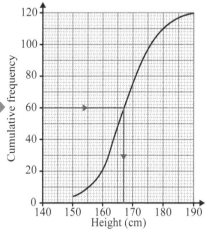

A cumulative frequency graph is a smooth curve. It shows you how many data values were **less than** a particular amount.

**Guided**

**(a)** Find an estimate for the median height.

**(1 mark)**

.......................... cm

Half the data values must be less than the median. There are 120 data values, so draw a line across from 60 on the vertical axis and down to the horizontal axis.

**(b)** Write true or false for each statement.
**A** The height of the tallest boy was 120 cm.

.......................

**B** The height of the shortest boy was 150 cm.

.......................

**C** More than half the boys were shorter than 170 cm.

.......................

**D** 20 boys were exactly 160 cm tall.

.......................   **(2 marks)**

**(c)** Show that 75% of the boys were shorter than 173 cm.   **(2 marks)**

For part (c), find 75% of 120. You can also use lines drawn on the graph to 'show' your working.

### Top exam tip!

Draw lines on your graph using a ruler and a sharp pencil to show any values you are reading off. Read graphs accurate to the nearest **small square**.

# 29 Probability

## Warm up

✓ For equally likely outcomes:

$$\text{Probability} = \frac{\text{number of successful outcomes}}{\text{total number of possible outcomes}}$$

✓ P(Event does not happen) = 1 − P(Event happens)

✓ For **independent** events: P(A and B) = P(A) × P(B)

✓ For **mutually exclusive** events: P(A or B) = P(A) + P(B)

✓ Venn diagrams can show probabilities or outcomes:

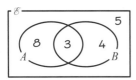

There are 8 + 3 = 11 outcomes in event A. There are 8 + 3 + 4 + 5 = 20 outcomes in the **whole sample space**.

So $P(A) = \frac{11}{20}$

✓ The event A ∩ B means A **and** B (or A **intersection** B)

$P(A \cap B) = \frac{3}{20}$

✓ The event A ∪ B means A **or** B (or A **union** B)

$P(A \cup B) = \frac{8 + 3 + 4}{20} = \frac{15}{20}$

## Reps

**1** A fair six-sided dice is thrown. Find the probability of getting

a 1     $\frac{1}{6}$

**a** an even number  ...........

**b** a square number  ...........

**c** a number less than 6  ...........

**d** a number more than 7  ...........

**2** A fair coin is tossed three times. Find the probability of getting

three heads     $\frac{1}{8}$

**a** three tails  ...........

**b** exactly two heads  ...........

**c** heads on the first toss  ...........

**d** tails on the first two tosses  ...........

**Links to:**
Pages
123–126

## Exam practice

**1.** A spinner can land on red or green or blue. The table shows the probabilities of landing on red or green.

| Colour | Red | Green | Blue |
|---|---|---|---|
| Probability | 0.2 | 0.5 | ....... |

The spinner is spun once.

**(a)** Work out the probability of landing on blue. **(1 mark)**

........................

The spinner is spun twice.

**(b)** Work out the probability of landing on the same colour twice. **(3 marks)**

P(Red-Red) = 0.2 × 0.2 = 0.04

P(Green-Green) = ...... × ...... = ......

P(Blue-Blue) = ..... × ...... = ......

P(same colour) = 0.04 + ...... + ......

........................

> The sum of all the possible outcomes of an event is 1

### Problem solved!

There are three ways of landing on the same colour:

Red-Red

Green-Green

Blue-Blue

**2.** $\mathscr{E}$ = {prime numbers less than 30}
$A$ = {2, 7, 11, 23}     $B$ = {3, 5, 7}

**(a)** Complete the Venn diagram to show this information.

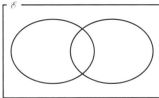

**(4 marks)**

A number is chosen at random from the universal set $\mathscr{E}$.

**(b)** Work out the probability that it is in the set $A \cup B$. **(2 marks)**

........................

> $\mathscr{E}$ represents the **universal set**. Every member of the universal set should appear **exactly once** on the Venn diagram.

In this case the numbers on the Venn diagram will represent the outcomes themselves, not the total number of possible outcomes.

### Top exam tip!

You don't have to simplify fractions when you are writing probabilities.

## 30 Conditional probability

**Warm up**

✓ P(A | B) means the probability that event A occurs **given that** event B has already occurred. This is called **conditional probability**. You can work it out from a Venn diagram by restricting the sample space.

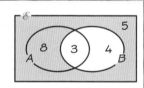

$P(A \mid B) = \dfrac{3}{3+4} = \dfrac{3}{7}$

✓ Tree diagrams can be used to show two or more events that happen one after the other.

✓ A probability tree diagram for **conditional** events will have different probabilities on each set of branches.

**Reps**

**1** For this Venn diagram, find

P(B | A)  $\dfrac{6}{17}$

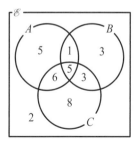

**a** P(A | C)  ............

**b** P(B | C)  ............

**c** P(A ∩ C | B)  ............

**d** P(A ∪ B | C)  ............

**2** The probability of a biased coin landing on heads is 0.4

Complete the tree diagram to show the possible outcomes when it is tossed twice.

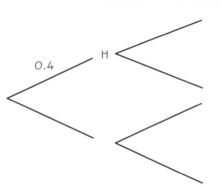

First toss     Second toss

## Exam practice

Links to:
Pages
127–128

A box contains 12 red counters and 8 blue counters.

Two counters are picked at random.

Anji draws a probability tree diagram for this information.

**Guided**

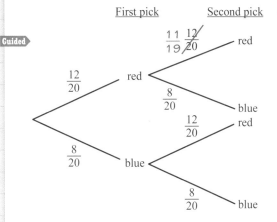

First pick          Second pick

$\frac{11}{19}\ \frac{12}{20}$ red

$\frac{12}{20}$ red

$\frac{8}{20}$ blue

$\frac{12}{20}$ red

$\frac{8}{20}$ blue

$\frac{8}{20}$ blue

When more than one item is selected **without replacement**, the probabilities change for the second pick.

### Problem solved!

Think about the branches of a tree diagram as different **parallel universes**. Along the top branch, a red counter is picked first. There are now 11 red counters left, and 19 counters in total, so the probability of picking a second red counter is $\frac{11}{19}$

**(a)** Write down **one** thing that is wrong with the probabilities in this tree diagram.

**(1 mark)**

.................................................................

.................................................................

**(b)** Cross out any incorrect probabilities and write the correct probabilities next to them. **(2 marks)**

**(c)** Find the probability that the two counters picked are the same colour. **(3 marks)**

### Top exam tip!

To find probabilities from a probability tree diagram you **multiply along** the branches then **add up** the outcomes.

.............................

## Workout 30 ☐

# 1 Number crunch

## Reps

**1** Circle any prime factors of the given number in each list.

**a**  20  4  ⑤  10  20

**b**  100  ②  ⑤  10  50

**c**  45  ③  ⑤  9  15

**2** Find the value of

**a**  $36^{\frac{1}{2}}$  6

**b**  $3^4$  81

**c**  $8^{-\frac{1}{3}}$  $\frac{1}{2}$

**3** Write as a single power of 5

**a**  $5^2 \div 25$  $5^0$

**b**  $(5^3)^2$  $5^6$

**c**  $25^5$  $5^{10}$

**4** Match up the equivalent surds.

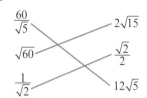

$\frac{60}{\sqrt{5}}$ — $12\sqrt{5}$

$\sqrt{60}$ — $2\sqrt{15}$

$\frac{1}{\sqrt{2}}$ — $\frac{\sqrt{2}}{2}$

## Exam practice

**1.** Write 96 as a product of its prime factors.

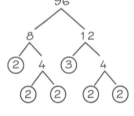

$96 = 2^5 \times 3$

**2.** Find the value of

**(a)** $25^{-\frac{1}{2}}$

$$25^{-\frac{1}{2}} = \frac{1}{25^{\frac{1}{2}}} = \frac{1}{5}$$

$\frac{1}{5}$

**(b)** $\left(\frac{8}{27}\right)^{\frac{2}{3}}$

$$\left(\frac{8}{27}\right)^{\frac{2}{3}} = \left(\frac{8^{\frac{1}{3}}}{27^{\frac{1}{3}}}\right)^2 = \left(\frac{2}{3}\right)^2 = \frac{4}{9}$$

$\frac{4}{9}$

**3.** Show that $\dfrac{\sqrt{12}-1}{2+\sqrt{3}}$ can be written in the form $p\sqrt{3} + q$, where $p$ and $q$ are integers.

$$\frac{\sqrt{12}-1}{2+\sqrt{3}} = \frac{\left(\sqrt{12}-1\right)\left(2-\sqrt{3}\right)}{\left(2+\sqrt{3}\right)\left(2-\sqrt{3}\right)}$$

$$= \frac{2\sqrt{12} - \sqrt{12}\sqrt{3} - 2 + \sqrt{3}}{4 - 2\sqrt{3} + 2\sqrt{3} - \sqrt{3}\sqrt{3}}$$

$$= \frac{4\sqrt{3} - 6 - 2 + \sqrt{3}}{4 - 3}$$

$$= 5\sqrt{3} - 8$$

# 2 Fractions, decimals and percentages

## Reps

**1** Work out

**a** $\frac{1}{2} + \frac{1}{4}$    $\frac{3}{4}$

**b** $1\frac{1}{2} \times \frac{3}{5}$    $\frac{9}{10}$

**c** $\frac{5}{6} \div \frac{3}{4}$    $1\frac{1}{9}$

**2** Circle the largest number in each list.

**a** 0.24   0.42   ⟨$\frac{1}{2}$⟩   $\frac{2}{5}$

**b** ⟨$0.2\dot{5}$⟩   0.25   $0.2\dot{5}$   $0.\dot{2}$

**c** ⟨$0.\dot{8}$⟩   $\frac{4}{5}$   $0.8\dot{5}$   0.85

**3** Write the correct multiplier.

**a** 50% increase   1.5

**b** 20% decrease   0.8

**c** 42% decrease   0.58

**4** Each amount has been increased by 35%. Find the original amounts.

**a** 67.5 g   50 g

**b** 2.43 m   1.8 m

**c** 1350 km   1000 km

## Exam practice

**1.** Work out $1\frac{1}{4} \times 2\frac{3}{5}$

Give your answer as a mixed number.

$$\frac{\cancel{5}}{4} \times \frac{13}{\cancel{5}} = \frac{13}{4} = 3\frac{1}{4}$$

$3\frac{1}{4}$
.......

**2.** $x = 0.2\dot{6}$

Prove algebraically that $x$ can be written as $\frac{4}{15}$

$10x = 2.6666...$
$100x = 26.6666...$
$90x = 100x - 10x$
$\quad = 24$
$x = \frac{24}{90} = \frac{4}{15}$

**3.** Jaden buys 20 bars of chocolate for a total of £7.95

She sells all 20 bars for 60p each.
Work out Jaden's percentage profit.

Total selling price:
20 × 0.6 = £12
Profit:
12 − 7.95 = £4.05
Percentage profit:
$\frac{4.05}{7.95} \times 100 = 50.943...\%$

50.9%
.......

# 3 Estimation and error

## Reps

**1** Round to 1 significant figure.

a   0.251    0.3

b   8.70    9

c   345    300

d   0.00372    0.004

**2** Each number has been rounded to 1 s.f. Find the upper bound.

a   500    550

b   8    8.5

c   0.002    0.0025

d   0.09    0.095

**3** Estimate the answer by rounding each number.

a   $5.5 \times 8.9$    54

b   $29.3 \div 4.5$    6

c   $7.75^2$    64

d   $391 \times 0.470$    200

**4** Write the missing number in each error interval.

a   $8500 \leqslant x < 9500$

b   $0.65 \leqslant x < 0.75$

c   $10.5 \leqslant x < 11.5$

d   $2.95 \leqslant x < 3.05$

## Exam practice

**1.** A number, $n$, is rounded to 1 decimal place. The result is 10.5

Write down the error interval for $n$.

$$10.45 \leqslant n < 10.55$$

**2.** Work out an estimate for

$$\frac{221 \times 5.2}{0.185}$$

$$\frac{200 \times 5}{0.2} = \frac{1000}{0.2} = \frac{10\,000}{2} = 5000$$

$$\underline{5000}$$

**3.** A mountain biker completes a course in 17 minutes, correct to the nearest minute. The course is 6.4 km long, correct to 1 decimal place.

Calculate the lower bound of the average speed of the mountain biker.

Give your answer in m/s correct to 2 decimal places.

| | Upper bound | Lower bound |
|---|---|---|
| Distance (m) | 6450 | 6350 |
| Time (s) | $17.5 \times 60$ $= 1050$ | $16.5 \times 60$ $= 990$ |

$$\text{Lower bound for speed} = \frac{6350}{1050}$$
$$= 6.047\ldots$$

$$\underline{6.05}\,\text{m/s}$$

# 4 Large and small numbers

## Reps

**1** Write in standard form.

| a | 29 000 | $2.9 \times 10^4$ |
| b | 0.05 | $5 \times 10^{-2}$ |
| c | 9 010 000 | $9.01 \times 10^6$ |
| d | 0.00006 | $6 \times 10^{-5}$ |

**2** Write as an ordinary number.

| a | $6.9 \times 10^{-1}$ | 0.69 |
| b | $8 \times 10^4$ | 80 000 |
| c | $2.03 \times 10^2$ | 203 |
| d | $5.5 \times 10^{-3}$ | 0.0055 |

**3** Find the number of different possible outcomes when each set of spinners is spun.

a  $5 \times 4 = 20$

b  $4 \times 3 \times 8 = 96$

c  $2 \times 3 \times 6 \times 4 = 144$

## Exam practice

**1.** Work out $(6.5 \times 10^6) \times (2 \times 10^{-13})$.
Give your answer in standard form.

$(6.5 \times 2) \times (10^6 \times 10^{-13}) = 13 \times 10^{-7}$

$\phantom{(6.5 \times 2) \times (10^6 \times 10^{-13})} = 1.3 \times 10^{-6}$
.................

**2.** Amy needs to choose a starter and a main course at a restaurant. A menu contains 7 different choices of starter and some main course options.

Amy says, 'There are exactly 80 different ways in which I could choose a starter and a main course.'

Is Amy correct? Give a reason for your answer.

$\dfrac{80}{7} = 11.428...$

There is no whole number that multiplies by 7 to give 80 so Amy could not be correct.

**3.** A combination lock consists of two letters from A to Z, followed by three digits from 0 to 9

Work out the total number of possible combinations. Give your answer in standard form.

$26 \times 26 \times 10 \times 10 \times 10 = 676000$

$\phantom{26 \times 26 \times 10 \times 10 \times 10} = 6.76 \times 10^5$

$\underline{6.76 \times 10^5}$
.................

# 5 Algebra essentials

## Reps

**1** Match the simplified expressions.

$4x \times 2xy^2$ ———— $8x^2y^2$

$2x^2y \times xy^2$ ———— $2xy$

$\dfrac{2x^2y}{x}$ ———— $4x^2y^3$

$x^2y \times 4y^2$ ———— $2x^3y^3$

**2** Find a pair of numbers with the given sum and product.

| | Sum | Product | Numbers |
|---|---|---|---|
| a | 8 | 7 | 7 and 1 |
| b | 3 | −4 | 4 and −1 |
| c | −2 | −15 | 3 and −5 |
| d | −6 | 9 | −3 and −3 |

**3** Expand and simplify

| a | $n(2 + n) + 3n$ | $5n + n^2$ |
| b | $(y + 2)(y - 4)$ | $y^2 - 2y - 8$ |
| c | $(3p + 5)(p - 2)$ | $3p^2 - p - 10$ |
| d | $(x^2 + 1)(x^2 - 1)$ | $x^4 - 1$ |

**4** Factorise

| a | $2x^3 - 4xy$ | $2x(x^2 - 2y)$ |
| b | $y^2 - 2y - 3$ | $(y + 1)(y - 3)$ |
| c | $3n^2 + 4n + 1$ | $(3n + 1)(n + 1)$ |
| d | $9a^2 - 4b^2$ | $(3a + 2b)(3a - 2b)$ |

## Exam practice

**1.** Factorise fully

(a) $4y^2 + 10y$

$= 2(2y^2 + 5y)$

$\phantom{=} = 2y(2y + 5)$

(b) $2x^2 + 5x - 3$

$\phantom{=} = (2x - 1)(x + 3)$

**2.** Expand and simplify

(a) $4(x - 1) + 5(2x + 3)$

$= 4x - 4 + 10x + 15$

$\phantom{=} = 14x + 11$

(b) $(n + 2)(n + 5)^2$

$= n(n + 5)^2 + 2(n + 5)^2$

$= n(n^2 + 10n + 25) + 2(n^2 + 10n + 25)$

$= n^3 + 10n^2 + 25n + 2n^2 + 20n + 50$

$\phantom{=} = n^3 + 12n^2 + 45n + 50$

**3.** The area of this rectangle is $8\,\text{cm}^2$.

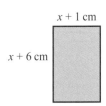

$x + 1$ cm

$x + 6$ cm

Show that $x^2 + 7x - 2 = 0$

Area $= (x + 1)(x + 6)$

$\phantom{\text{Area }} = x^2 + x + 6x + 6$

$\phantom{\text{Area }} = x^2 + 7x + 6$

$x^2 + 7x + 6 = 8$

$x^2 + 7x - 2 = 0$

# 6 Formulae and equations

## Reps

**1** Solve

**a** $10x - 10 = 60$    $x = 7$

**b** $2x + 1 = 6x - 9$    $x = 2.5$

**c** $8 - 8x = 20 - 2x$    $x = -2$

**d** $\dfrac{x}{6} + \dfrac{x}{3} = 5$    $x = 10$

**2** Write 'expression', 'equation' or 'formula'.

**a** $10x^2 - 1$    expression

**b** $p = 2q + 1$    formula

**c** $x = 2x - 5$    equation

**d** $2y = 8$    equation

**3** Substitute into the formula

$$F = \frac{x^2 - 2y}{z}$$

|   | $x$ | $y$ | $z$ | $F$ |
|---|-----|-----|-----|-----|
| **a** | 2 | 1 | 1 | 2 |
| **b** | 5 | 5 | 5 | 3 |
| **c** | 10 | 10 | -4 | -20 |

**4** Make $Q$ the subject of each formula.

**a** $P = Q + 50$    $Q = P - 50$

**b** $P = \dfrac{Q + 1}{5}$    $Q = 5P - 1$

**c** $P = 2QR + 5$    $Q = \dfrac{P - 5}{2R}$

## Exam practice

**1.** Find the area of this square.

3x − 5 cm

x + 2 cm

$3x - 5 = x + 2$
$3x = x + 7$
$2x = 7$
$x = 3.5$
Side length = 5.5
So area = 30.25 cm²    <u>30.25</u> cm²

**2.** Solve $\dfrac{2x + 1}{3} = x - 7$

$2x + 1 = 3(x - 7)$
$2x + 1 = 3x - 21$
$2x + 22 = 3x$
$22 = x$

$x = \underline{22}$

**3.** The following formula can be used to estimate the power generated by a wind turbine.

$$F = \frac{D^2 \times W^3}{60}$$

where $P$ is the power generated in watts, $D$ is the diameter of the blade in metres, $W$ is the wind speed in mph.
Supraj says that a wind turbine with a diameter of 4 m generates more than 500 watts of power when the wind is blowing at 12 mph.
Is Supraj correct? Show your working.

$$P = \frac{4^2 \times 12^3}{60} = \frac{27\,648}{60} = 460.8$$

460.8 is less than 500 so Supraj is wrong.

# 7 Sequences

## Reps

**1** Find the next two terms in each sequence.

| a | −1 | 4 | 9 | 14 | 19 | 24 | 29 |
| b | 15 | 11 | 7 | 3 | −1 | −5 | −9 |
| c | 1 | 2 | 3 | 5 | 8 | 13 | 21 |
| d | 1 | 2 | 4 | 7 | 11 | 16 | 22 |

**2** Write the first three terms in the sequences with these $n$th terms.

| a | $3n + 10$ | 13 | 16 | 19 |
| b | $20 - 2n$ | 18 | 16 | 14 |
| c | $2n^2 - 5$ | −3 | 3 | 13 |
| d | $3n^2 - n + 1$ | 3 | 11 | 25 |

**3** Find the $n$th term of each arithmetic sequence.

| a | 10 | 15 | 20 | 25 | 30 | $5n + 5$ |
| b | −1 | 5 | 11 | 17 | 23 | $6n - 7$ |
| c | 13 | 7 | 1 | −5 | −11 | $-6n + 19$ |
| d | 1 | 10 | 19 | 28 | 37 | $9n - 8$ |

**4** Fill in the differences and second differences in this quadratic sequence, then work out the $n$th term.

$$
\begin{array}{ccccccccc}
& 5 & & 9 & & 15 & & 23 & & 33 \\
\text{First} & & +4 & & +6 & & +8 & & +10 \\
\text{Second} & & & +2 & & +2 & & +2 \\
\end{array}
$$

$n$th term $= n^2 + n + 3$

## Exam practice

**1.** The $n$th term in a sequence is $6n - 1$
Is 103 a term in this sequence?
Show how you get your answer.

$6n - 1 = 103$
$\quad 6n = 104$
$\quad\quad n = 17.33\ldots$

Not an integer, so 103 is not a term in the sequence.

**2.** The rule to get from one term to the next term in a sequence is

Add $k$ then multiply by 2

The third term is 52 and the fourth term is 112
Find the first term in the sequence.

$2(52 + k) = 112$
$\quad 52 + k = 56$
$\quad\quad\quad k = 4$

$52 \div 2 = 26$ and $26 - 4 = 22$ (term 2)
$22 \div 2 = 11$ and $11 - 4 = 7$ (term 1)

First term in sequence is 7

**3.** Here are the first five terms of a sequence.

$$
\begin{array}{ccccccccc}
4 & & 14 & & 30 & & 52 & & 80 \\
& +10 & & +16 & & +22 & & +28 \\
& & +6 & & +6 & & +6 \\
\end{array}
$$

Find an expression, in terms of $n$, for the $n$th term of this sequence.

| $n$ | 1 | 2 | 3 | 4 | 5 |
|---|---|---|---|---|---|
| $u_n$ | 4 | 14 | 30 | 52 | 80 |
| $3n^2$ | 3 | 12 | 27 | 48 | 75 |
| $u_n - 3n^2$ | 1 | 2 | 3 | 4 | 5 |

$n$th term $= 3n^2 + n$

$3n^2 + n$

# 8 Straight-line graphs

**1** Write down the gradient and $y$-intercept of each line.

| | Equation | Gradient | $y$-int |
|---|---|---|---|
| a | $y = -2x + 5$ | $-2$ | $(0, 5)$ |
| b | $y = \frac{1}{2}x - 3$ | $\frac{1}{2}$ | $(0, -3)$ |
| c | $y = 11 - x$ | $-1$ | $(0, 11)$ |
| d | $3x + y = 4$ | $-3$ | $(0, 4)$ |

**2** Find the equation of the line through each pair of points.

| | Points | Equation |
|---|---|---|
| a | $(0, 1)$ and $(2, 5)$ | $y = 2x + 1$ |
| b | $(0, 10)$ and $(4, -2)$ | $y = -3x + 10$ |
| c | $(3, 5)$ and $(7, 3)$ | $y = -0.5x + 6.5$ |
| d | $(-2, 0)$ and $(1, 12)$ | $y = 4x + 8$ |

**3** Find the equation of the line that is parallel to $y = 3x - 1$ and passes through the given point.

| | Points | Equation |
|---|---|---|
| a | $(0, -2)$ | $y = 3x - 2$ |
| b | $(0, 0)$ | $y = 3x$ |
| c | $(1, 5)$ | $y = 3x + 2$ |
| d | $(-2, -2)$ | $y = 3x + 4$ |

**4** Match up the pairs of perpendicular lines.

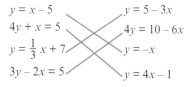

$y = x - 5$     $y = 5 - 3x$
$4y + x = 5$     $4y = 10 - 6x$
$y = \frac{1}{3}x + 7$     $y = -x$
$3y - 2x = 5$     $y = 4x - 1$

**1.** Lines **A** and **B** are parallel. The point $(10, q)$ is on line **A**. Line **B** cuts the $y$-axis at $(0, q)$.

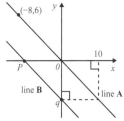

Find the coordinates of the point $P$ where line **B** crosses the $x$-axis.

Gradient of line **A** $= \dfrac{-6}{8} = -\dfrac{3}{4}$

Equation of line **A**: $y = -\dfrac{3}{4}x$

When $x = 10$ on line **A**, $y = -7.5$

Equation of line **B**: $y = -\dfrac{3}{4}x - 7.5$

When $y = 0$ on line **B**, $x = -10$

$$P = (-10, 0)$$

**2.** The points $P(1, 3)$, $Q(10, 0)$ and $R(3, k)$ form the vertices of a right-angled triangle. $QPR$ is the right angle. Find an equation of the straight line that passes through $R$ and $Q$.

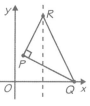

Gradient of $PQ = \dfrac{-3}{9} = -\dfrac{1}{3}$

So gradient of $PR = 3$
Move 2 across so move $2 \times 3 = 6$ up
Coordinates of $R = (3, 9)$

Gradient of $RQ = \dfrac{-9}{7} = -\dfrac{9}{7}$

Substitute $x = 10$, $y = 0$ into $y = mx + c$:

$0 = -\dfrac{9}{7} \times 10 + c$    so $c = \dfrac{90}{7}$

So equation of $RQ$ is $y = -\dfrac{9}{7}x + \dfrac{90}{7}$

# 9 Quadratic equations

**1** Write down the answers to each factorised quadratic equation.

**a** $(x-4)(x-3) = 0$    $x = 4$ or $3$

**b** $(x+2)(x+2) = 0$    $x = -2$

**c** $(2x+1)(x-7) = 0$    $x = -\dfrac{1}{2}$ or $7$

**d** $(x+4)(3x-2) = 0$    $x = -4$ or $\dfrac{2}{3}$

**3** Rearrange into the form $ax^2 + bx + c$.

**a** $x^2 = 2 - 6x$    $x^2 + 6x - 2 = 0$

**b** $5x = 2x^2 + 1$    $2x^2 - 5x + 1 = 0$

**c** $x + 1 = 2x^2 - 2$    $2x^2 - x - 3 = 0$

**d** $x(x+5) = 3x^2$    $2x^2 - 5x = 0$

**2** Find the missing numbers to complete the square.

**a** $x^2 + 6x + 2 = (x+3)^2 - 7$

**b** $x^2 - 8x - 5 = (x-4)^2 - 21$

**c** $x^2 + 2x - 1 = (x+1)^2 - 2$

**d** $x^2 - 10x + 10 = (x-5)^2 - 15$

**4** Use the quadratic formula to solve, correct to 1 decimal place.

**a** $x^2 - 6x + 2 = 0$    $x = 5.6$ or $0.4$

**b** $2x^2 + 10x + 1 = 0$    $x = -4.9$ or $-0.1$

**c** $3x^2 - 6x + 2 = 0$    $x = 1.6$ or $0.4$

**d** $x^2 - x - 7 = 0$    $x = 3.2$ or $-2.2$

## Exam practice

**1.** Solve $x^2 - 8x - 1 = 0$

Write your answer in the form $a \pm \sqrt{b}$, where $a$ and $b$ are integers.

$$x^2 - 8x - 1 = 0$$
$$(x-4)^2 - 16 - 1 = 0$$
$$(x-4)^2 - 17 = 0$$
$$(x-4)^2 = 17$$
$$x - 4 = \pm\sqrt{17}$$
$$x = 4 \pm \sqrt{17}$$

$$x = \underline{4} \pm \sqrt{\underline{17}}$$

**2.** The diagram shows two right-angled triangles.

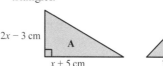

2x – 3 cm    **A**    x cm    **B**

x + 5 cm      3 cm

The ratio of the area of triangle **A** to the area of triangle **B** is $2:1$

Find the value of $x$.

Area of A = 2 × area of B

$$\frac{1}{2}(2x-3)(x+5) = 2 \times \frac{1}{2}(3x)$$

$$\frac{1}{2}(2x^2 - 3x + 10x - 15) = 3x$$

$$2x^2 + 7x - 15 = 6x$$
$$2x^2 + x - 15 = 0$$
$$(2x-5)(x+3) = 0$$

$$x = \frac{5}{2} \text{ or } -3$$

$$x = \underline{\frac{5}{2}}$$

# 10 Curvy graphs

**1** For each quadratic graph, find the coordinates of the turning point.

**a** $y = (x + 1)^2 - 6$    (–1, –6)

**b** $y = x^2 + 4$    (0, 4)

**c** $y = (x - 10)^2$    (10, 0)

**d** $y = x^2 - 2x + 3$    (1, 2)

**2** Match each graph to the correct equation.

$x^2 + y^2 = 6$                $y = 10 - x^2$                $y = x^3 + x^2$

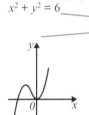
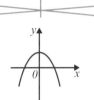
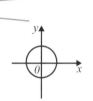

## Exam practice

**1. (a)** On the grid draw the graph of
$y = x^2 + 2x - 1$

You can use the table of values to
help you.

| $x$ | –3 | –2 | –1 | 0 | 1 |
|---|---|---|---|---|---|
| $y$ | 2 | –1 | –2 | –1 | 2 |

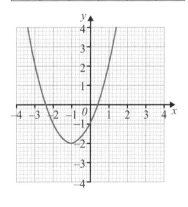

**(b)** Write down the coordinates of the turning point of the graph.

(–1, –2)

**(c)** Write down the solutions to
$x^2 + 2x - 1 = 1$

$x = 0.7$ or $-2.7$

**2.** Find the equation of the tangent to the circle $x^2 + y^2 = 20$ at the point (4, 2).

Gradient of radius $= \dfrac{2}{4} = \dfrac{1}{2}$

So gradient of tangent $= -2$

$y = mx + c$

$2 = -2(4) + c$

So $c = 10$

$y = -2x + 10$

# 11 Simultaneous equations

## Reps

**1** Multiply every term in each linear equation by 2

| a | $x - 4y = 2$ | $2x - 8y = 4$ |
|---|---|---|
| b | $3x + 5y = 7$ | $6x + 10y = 14$ |
| c | $2x = 6y + 1$ | $4x = 12y + 2$ |
| d | $y = 3 - x$ | $2y = 6 - 2x$ |

**2** Substitute $y = 3x + 1$ into each expression and simplify.

| a | $5x - y$ | $2x - 1$ |
|---|---|---|
| b | $x - 3y + 1$ | $-8x - 2$ |
| c | $x^2 + y^2$ | $10x^2 + 6x + 1$ |
| d | $xy - 2x + 7$ | $3x^2 - x + 7$ |

**3** Solve each pair of simultaneous equations.

| a | $2x - y = 1$ |
|---|---|
|   | $3x + 2y = 19$ |
|   | |
|   | $x = 3$ |
|   | $y = 5$ |

| b | $y = 2 - x$ |
|---|---|
|   | $y^2 = x + 4$ |
|   | |
|   | $x = 0$ $x = 5$ |
|   | $y = 2$ $y = -3$ |

| c | $4x - 3y = 5$ |
|---|---|
|   | $2x + 5y = 9$ |
|   | |
|   | $x = 2$ |
|   | $y = 1$ |

## Exam practice

**1.** Solve the simultaneous equations

$$x + y = 6 \qquad (1)$$
$$2x - 4y = 3 \qquad (2)$$
$$2 \times (1): 2x + 2y = 12 \qquad (3)$$
$$(3) - (2): 2x + 2y - (2x - 4y) = 12 - 3$$
$$6y = 9$$
$$y = 1.5$$

Substitute into $(1)$:
$$x + 1.5 = 6$$
$$x = 4.5$$

$$x = \underline{4.5}$$
$$y = \underline{1.5}$$

**2.** A circle has the equation $x^2 + y^2 = 16$

A straight line has the equation $y - 2x = 8$

Find the coordinates of the points where the circle and the line intersect.

$$x^2 + y^2 = 16 \qquad (1)$$
$$y - 2x = 8 \qquad (2)$$

Rearrange $(2)$: $y = 2x + 8$ $\qquad (3)$

Substitute $(3)$ into $(1)$:
$$x^2 + (2x + 8)^2 = 16$$
$$x^2 + 4x^2 + 32x + 64 = 16$$
$$5x^2 + 32x + 48 = 0$$
$$(5x + 12)(x + 4) = 0$$
$$x = -2.4 \text{ or } -4$$

When $x = -2.4$, $y = 2 \times (-2.4) + 8$
$$= 3.2$$

When $x = -4$, $y = 2 \times (-4) + 8 = 0$

$(\underline{-2.4}, \underline{3.2})$ and $(\underline{-4}, \underline{0})$

# 12 Inequalities

**1** Write down all the integers that satisfy each inequality.

**a** $3 < x < 7$     4, 5, 6

**b** $-5 \leqslant x < -3$     –5, –4

**c** $0 \leqslant x \leqslant 3$     0, 1, 2, 3

**d** $10 < x < 15$     11, 12, 13, 14

**2** Solve each inequality.

**a** $x + 1 \geqslant 2x + 5$     $x \leqslant -4$

**b** $3x - 2 \leqslant 10$     $x \leqslant 4$

**c** $5 - x > 8 - 2x$     $x > 3$

**d** $x^2 - 1 < 0$     $-1 < x < 1$

**3** Write down the inequality represented by each shaded region.

**a** $y \leqslant 3$     **b** $y < -x$     **c** $y \geqslant 2x - 5$     **d** $x > 2$

**1.** On the grid, shade the region that satisfies all of these inequalities.

$y \leqslant 3$     $y > 1 - x$     $y \geqslant 2x - 4$

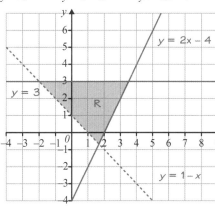

Label the region **R**.

**2.** Solve the inequality $x^2 - 1 > 2(x + 1)$.

$x^2 - 1 > 2x + 2$

$x^2 - 2x - 3 > 0$

$(x + 1)(x - 3) > 0$

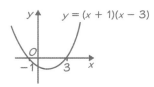

So the solution is $x < -1$ or $x > 3$

# 13 Applications of algebra

## Reps

**1** Assuming $k$ is an integer, write odd or even for each expression.

**a** $10k$      even

**b** $k(k + 1)$      even

**c** $4k + 5$      odd

**d** $k + (k + 3)$      odd

**2** Work out the discriminant of each quadratic expression.

**a** $x^2 + 2x + 1$      0

**b** $x^2 - 5x + 3$      13

**c** $3x^2 - x - 5$      61

**d** $2x^2 - 1$      8

**3** Match each $y = ax^2 + bx + c$ curve to the correct discriminant.

$b^2 - 4ac > 0$        $b^2 - 4ac = 0$        $b^2 - 4ac < 0$

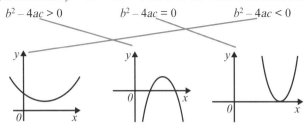

## Exam practice

**1.** $n$ is an integer.

Prove algebraically that $\frac{1}{2}(2n - 1)^2 + \frac{1}{2}(2n + 1)^2$ is always an odd number.

$\frac{1}{2}(2n - 1)^2 + \frac{1}{2}(2n + 1)^2$

$= \frac{1}{2}(4n^2 - 4n + 1) + \frac{1}{2}(4n^2 + 4n + 1)$

$= 2n^2 - 2n + \frac{1}{2} + 2n^2 + 2n + \frac{1}{2}$

$= 4n^2 + 1$

This is EVEN + ODD so it must be an odd number.

**2.** The straight line with equation $y = 6 - x$ is a tangent to the circle with equation $x^2 + y^2 = k$.

Find the value of $k$.

$y = 6 - x$        ①

$x^2 + y^2 = k$        ②

Substitute ① into ②:

$x^2 + (6 - x)^2 = k$

$x^2 + 36 - 12x + x^2 = k$

$2x^2 - 12x + 36 - k = 0$

Discriminant: $b^2 - 4ac = 0$

$(-12)^2 - 4 \times 2 \times (36 - k) = 0$

$144 - 288 + 8k = 0$

$8k = 144$

$k = 18$

$k = \underline{18}$

# 14 Functions

**1** $f(x) = x^2$ and $g(x) = 1 - 4x$
Evaluate

**a** $f(-2)$     4

**b** $g(-3)$     13

**c** $g(2)$     −7

**d** $fg(2)$     49

**2** $f(x) = 2x + 1$
Write down an expression for

**a** $f(x + 2)$     $2x + 5$

**b** $f(x^2)$     $2x^2 + 1$

**c** $ff(x)$     $4x + 3$

**d** $f^{-1}(x)$     $\dfrac{x - 1}{2}$

**3** Sketch the transformation shown.

**a** $y = f(x + 3)$      **b** $y = -f(x)$      **c** $y = f(-x)$

**1.** The functions f and g are such that
$f(x) = 2(x - 5)$ and $g(x) = \dfrac{x}{3} - 1$

**(a)** Find the value of g(30)

$$\frac{30}{3} - 1 = 10 - 1 = 9$$

$g(30) = \underline{9}$

**(b)** Find $f^{-1}(x)$

$$y = 2(x - 5)$$
$$y = 2x - 10$$
$$y + 10 = 2x$$
$$\frac{y + 10}{2} = 2x$$

$f^{-1}(x) = \dfrac{x + 10}{2}$

**(c)** Find $ff(x)$

$$ff(x) = f(2(x - 5))$$
$$= 2(2(x - 5) - 5)$$
$$= 2(2x - 15)$$

$ff(x) = \underline{4x - 30}$

**2.** The grid shows the graph with equation
$y = f(x)$. On the same grid, sketch the
graph with equation $y = -f(x + 2)$.

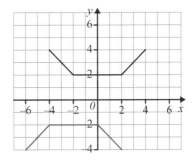

# 15 Gradient and area

## Reps

**1** Estimate the gradient of the curve at each point.

**a** $A$  –0.6

**b** $B$  1.6

**c** $C$  0

**d** $D$  –0.4

Answers can vary by ± 0.2

**2** Use strips 0.5 wide to estimate the area under the curve between

**a** 0.5 and 1      0.925

**b** –1.5 and –1    0.55

**c** –1 and 0      0.65

**d** –1 and 1      2.4

Answers can vary by ± 0.2

## Exam practice

**1.** A robotic vacuum cleaner travels down a hallway. It moves at 0.1 m/s for the first 2 minutes. It then stops at a charging station for 1 minute, before returning in 4 minutes.

Draw a travel graph for this journey.

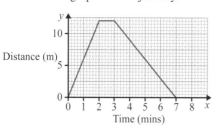

**2.** Here is a speed–time graph for a car.

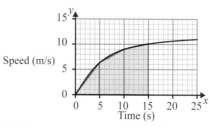

**(a)** Work out an estimate for the distance travelled by the car in the first 15 seconds.

$\frac{1}{2}(5 \times 6.5) + \frac{1}{2} \times 5(6.5 + 9)$

$+ \frac{1}{2} \times 5(9 + 10)$

$= 102.5$

102.5 m

**(b)** Is your answer an overestimate or an underestimate? Give a reason for your answer.

An underestimate as all trapeziums are underneath the curve.

# 16 Ratio and proportion

## Reps

**1** Write these ratios in simplest form.

**a**  5:10          1:2

**b**  25:10          5:2

**c**  12:30:15          4:10:5

**3** $y$ is directly proportional to $x$.
When $y = 3$, $x = 10$
Find

**a**  $y$ when $x = 5$          1.5

**b**  $x$ when $y = 15$          50

**c**  $y$ when $x = 8$          2.4

**2** Divide £600 in the following ratios.

**a**  1:3          £150 and £450

**b**  5:1          £500 and £100

**c**  1:9          £60 and £540

**4** 12 kg of potatoes cost £9.12
Find the cost of the following amounts.

**a**  1 kg          76p

**b**  5 kg          £3.80

**c**  750 g          57p

## Exam practice

**1.** A bag contains solid balls and hollow balls. They are all either red or white.

- The ratio of red to white balls is 2:1

- The ratio of the number of solid red balls to the number of hollow red balls is 9:11

- The ratio of the number of solid white balls to the number of hollow white balls is 3:7

Work out what fraction of all the balls are solid.

$\frac{2}{3}$ of all the balls are red.

$\frac{9}{20} \times \frac{2}{3} = \frac{3}{10}$ are solid and red.

$\frac{3}{10} \times \frac{1}{3} = \frac{1}{10}$ are solid and white.

$\frac{3}{10} + \frac{1}{10} = \frac{4}{10}$ are solid.

$\frac{2}{5}$
....

**2.** $y$ is directly proportional to $x^2$
$y = 1600$ when $x = 20$

Find the value of $y$ when $x = 25$

$y = kx^2$

$1600 = k \times 20^2$

$k = 1600 \div 400 = 4$

$y = 4x^2$

$\phantom{y} = 4 \times 25^2$

$\phantom{y} = 2500$

$y = \underline{2500}$

# 17 Compound measures

**1** Convert

a  65 cm into m    0.65 m

b  0.15 litres into ml    150 ml

c  2400 g into kg    2.4 kg

d  420 m into km    0.42 km

**2** A cyclist travels 30 km. Work out her average speed if she takes

a  6 hours    5 km/h

b  2.5 hours    12 km/h

c  90 minutes    20 km/h

d  $1\frac{1}{4}$ hours    24 km/h

**3** Complete the missing values in the table.

| | Mass (g) | Volume (cm³) | Density (g/cm³) |
|---|---|---|---|
| a | 100 | 8 | 12.5 |
| b | 660 | 300 | 2.2 |
| c | 400 | 250 | 1.6 |

**4** Convert

a  0.8 m² into cm²    8000 cm²

b  300 mm³ into cm³    0.3 cm³

c  0.025 km² into m²    25 000 m²

d  0.004 m³ into cm³    4000 cm³

## Exam practice

**1.** An iron block has a mass of 22.8 kg. The density of iron is 7.9 g/cm³.

Work out the volume of the block. Give your answer correct to 3 significant figures.

Mass = 22.8 × 1000 = 22 800 grams

$V = \dfrac{M}{D} = \dfrac{22800}{7.9} = 2886.075...$

2890 cm³

**2.** Two friends drove at constant speeds on the M8 from Glasgow to Edinburgh.

Hamid took $1\frac{1}{2}$ hours to complete the 75 km journey. Chloe started her journey 15 minutes after Hamid, and caught up with him 45 minutes later.

Work out Chloe's speed.

Hamid's speed $= \dfrac{D}{T} = \dfrac{75}{1.5}$

$= 50$ km/h

After 1 hour he had travelled 50 km

Chloe's speed $= \dfrac{D}{T} = \dfrac{50}{0.75}$

$= 66.6666...$

66.7 km/h

# 18 Growth and decay

**1** If $P = 200 \times 0.8^n$, find $P$ when

| a | $n = 1$ | 160 |
| b | $n = 3$ | 102.4 |
| c | $n = 0$ | 200 |
| d | $n = 5$ | 65.536 |

**2** Complete this table showing 5% per annum compound interest.

| Initial amount | £2000 |
|---|---|
| End of year 1 | £2100 |
| End of year 2 | £2205 |
| End of year 3 | £2315.25 |
| End of year 4 | £2431.01 |

**3** Match each equation to the correct line.

| a | $y = 3^x$ | b | $y = 2^{-x}$ | c | $y = 1.5^x$ | d | $y = \left(\frac{3}{4}\right)^x$ |
|---|---|---|---|---|---|---|---|
|  | A |  | E |  | C |  | D |

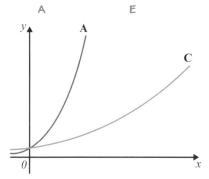

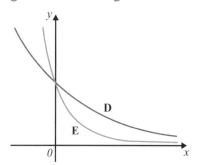

**Exam practice**

**1.** Poppy and Suresh each buy a used car. Poppy's car cost £2400 and will depreciate by 10% each year. Suresh's car cost £3500 and will depreciate by 15% each year.

Whose car will be worth more after 5 years?

You must show all your working.

Poppy: $2400 \times 0.9^n$

Value after 5 years $= 2400 \times 0.9^5$

$= £1417.18$

Suresh: $3500 \times 0.85^n$

Value after 5 years $= 3500 \times 0.85^5$

$= £1552.97$

So Suresh's car will be worth more.

**2.** Alison has invested £1800 in a savings account. The account earns $p\%$ compound interest per annum.

After 4 years, her investment is worth £1986.86

Work out the value of $p$.

$1800 \times x^4 = 1986.86$

$x^4 = 1.103\,81\ldots$

$x = 1.025$

This is the multiplier for a 2.5% increase.

$p = \underline{2.5}$

# 19 All the angles

Reps

**1** Write in the missing angles on this diagram.

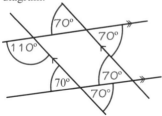

**2** Write in the missing angles on this diagram.

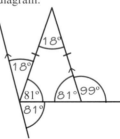

**3** Complete the missing values in the table showing angles in regular polygons.

| | Number of sides | Interior angle | Exterior angle |
|---|---|---|---|
| a | 8 | 135° | 45° |
| b | 20 | 162° | 18° |
| c | 10 | 144° | 36° |

Exam practice

**1.** In the diagram, *ABFE* is a parallelogram, and *BCD* is a straight line.

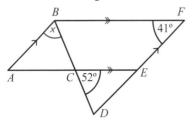

Show that angle *ABC* = 87°

Angle ACB = 52°

Reason: Vertically opposite angles are equal.

Angle BAC = 41°

Reason: Opposite angles in a parallelogram are equal.

So 52° + 41° + x = 180°

Reason: Angles in a triangle add up to 180°

x = 180° − 93° = 87°

**2.** This pattern is made from identical regular polygons **A**, and equilateral triangles.

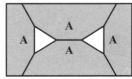

Work out the number of sides of polygon **A**.

If *x* is interior angle of A:

x + x + 60° = 360°

2x = 300°

x = 150°

Exterior angle of A = 180° − 150° = 30°

$\frac{360°}{n} = 30°$, so $n = \frac{360°}{30°} = 12$

A has 12 sides.

# 20 Trigonometry

**1** Find the sizes of the missing angles to 1 decimal place.

**a**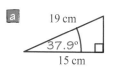

**b**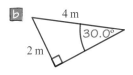

**c**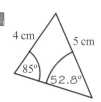

**2** Find the missing side lengths.

**a**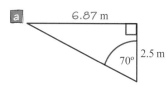

**b**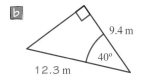

**c**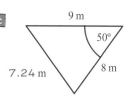

## Exam practice

**1.** *ADC* and *ABC* are triangles. Angle *ABC* is a right angle.

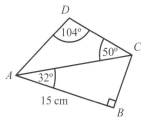

Find the length of *AD*. Give your answer correct to 1 decimal place.

$\cos 32° = \dfrac{15}{AC}$ so AC = 17.6876... cm

$\dfrac{\sin 50°}{AD} = \dfrac{\sin 104°}{17.6876...}$

$AD = \dfrac{17.6876}{\sin 104°} \times \sin 50°$

$= 13.9643...$ cm

$\underline{14.0}$ cm

**2.** The table shows values of *x* and *y* that satisfy the equation $y = a + b \cos x°$.

| x | 0 | 45 | 90 |
|---|---|---|---|
| y | 5 | $3 + \sqrt{2}$ | 3 |

Find the exact value of *y* when *x* = 30

$\cos 0° = 1$  so $a + b \times 1 = 5$

$a + b = 5$

$\cos 90° = 0$  so $a + b \times 0 = 3$

$a = 3$

$a = 3$ and $b = 2$

So $y = a + b \cos 30°$

$= 3 + 2 \times \dfrac{\sqrt{3}}{2}$

$= 3 + \sqrt{3}$

# 21 Length, area and volume

## Reps

**1** Find the missing lengths in these triangles.

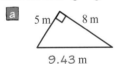

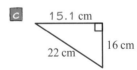

**2** Find the areas or volumes of these shapes and solids.

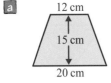

A = 240 cm²

A = 46.5 cm²

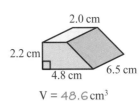

V = 48.6 cm³

## Exam practice

**1.** The diagram shows a cuboid.

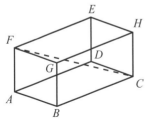

$AB$ = 11 cm and $BC$ = 16 cm.
The diagonal $FC$ = 21 cm.
Calculate the volume of the cuboid.

$$11^2 + 16^2 + AF^2 = 21^2$$
$$AF = \sqrt{64}$$
$$AF = 8$$
$$\text{Volume} = 11 \times 16 \times 8 = 1408$$
$$\underline{1408}\text{ cm}^3$$

**2.** The diagram shows a triangle.

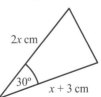

The area of this triangle is 35 cm².
Find the value of $x$.

$$\text{Area} = \frac{1}{2}\,ab\sin C$$
$$35 = \frac{1}{2}(2x)\,(x + 3)\,\sin 30°$$
$$35 = \frac{x(x + 3)}{2}$$
$$70 = x^2 + 3x$$
$$x^2 + 3x - 70 = 0$$
$$(x + 10)(x - 7) = 0$$
$$x = -10 \text{ or } x = 7$$

$$x = \underline{7}\text{ cm}^2$$

# 22 Circles, sectors and cylinders

## Reps

**1** Work out the missing values for these cylinders.

**a**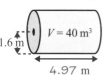

$V = 40$ m³
1.6 m
4.97 m

**b**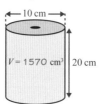

10 cm
$V = 1570$ cm³ | 20 cm

**c**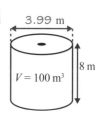

3.99 m
8 m
$V = 100$ m³

**2** Find the area of each sector and the length of the arc $AB$.

**a**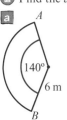

A
140°
6 m
B

**b**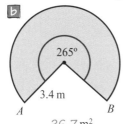

265°
3.4 m
A          B

**c**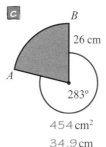

B
26 cm
A
283°

Area = 44.0 m²          26.7 m²          454 cm²
Arc length = 14.7 m     15.7 m           34.9 cm

## Exam practice

**1.** The diagram shows a sector of a circle.

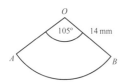

O
105°  14 mm
A          B

Find its perimeter.

Arc length = $\dfrac{x}{360°} \times 2\pi r$

$= \dfrac{105°}{360°} \times 2\pi \times 14$

$= 25.656...$

Perimeter = 25.7 + 14 + 14 = 53.7

<u>53.7</u> mm

**2.** A paperweight is made in the shape of a solid hemisphere.

Volume of sphere = $\dfrac{4}{3}\pi r^3$
Surface area of a sphere = $4\pi r^2$

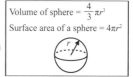

r

The total surface area of the hemisphere is $48\pi$ cm². Find the exact volume of the hemisphere.

Give your answer in terms of $\pi$.

Total hemisphere SA = $\pi r^2 + \dfrac{1}{2}(4\pi r^2)$

$= 3\pi r^2$

$48\pi = 3\pi r^2$ so $r = 4$

Vol. hemisphere = $\dfrac{1}{2}\left(\dfrac{4}{3}\pi \times 4^3\right) = \dfrac{128}{3}\pi$

<u>$\dfrac{128}{3}\pi$</u> cm³

# 23 Transformations

**1** On the grid, transform **T** by:

**B**: rotation 90° clockwise about *O*

**C**: enlargement centre *O* with scale factor 2

**D**: translation by vector $\begin{pmatrix} 0 \\ 5 \end{pmatrix}$

**E**: enlargement centre *O* with scale factor –1

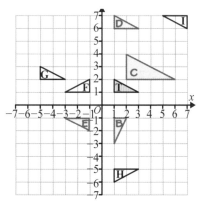

**2** Describe the transformation from **T** to:

**G**: translation by vector $\begin{pmatrix} -6 \\ 1 \end{pmatrix}$

**H**: reflection in line $y = -2$
**I**: rotation 180° about (4, 4)

1.

**(a)** Rotate shape **R** 180° about the origin. Label the new shape **A**.

**(b)** Translate shape **R** by the vector $\begin{pmatrix} -1 \\ 4 \end{pmatrix}$. Label the new shape **B**.

2. Complete each statement.

**(a)** A translation by vector $\begin{pmatrix} 2 \\ 5 \end{pmatrix}$ followed by a translation by vector $\begin{pmatrix} -3 \\ 1 \end{pmatrix}$ is the same as a translation by vector $\begin{pmatrix} -1 \\ 6 \end{pmatrix}$.

**(b)** An enlargement scale factor 3 with centre *O* followed by an enlargement scale factor $\frac{1}{2}$ with centre *O* is the same as an enlargement scale factor 1.5 with centre *O*.

# 24 Similar and congruent

**Reps**

**1** Find the missing lengths in each pair of similar shapes.

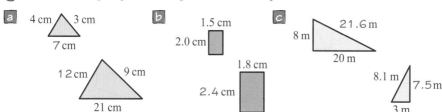

**2** Write down the condition that shows that each pair of triangles is congruent.

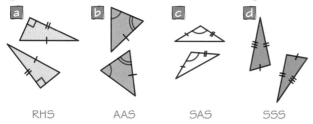

RHS          AAS          SAS          SSS

**Exam practice**

**1.** Two cylinders **A** and **B** are mathematically similar. The ratio of the surface area of cylinder **A** to the surface area of cylinder **B** is $25:64$

The volume of cylinder **A** is $20\,cm^3$.
Show that the volume of cylinder **B** is $81.92\,cm^3$.

$$25 \times k^2 = 64$$

$$k^2 = \frac{64}{25}$$

$$k = 1.6$$

Volume of B $= 20 \times 1.6^3$
$= 81.92\,cm^3$

**2.** The two rectangles shown in this diagram are similar.

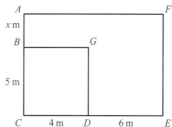

Find the **two** possible values of $x$.

Option 1

$$\frac{BC}{CD} = \frac{AC}{CE}$$

$$\frac{5}{4} = \frac{x+5}{10}$$

$$x = \frac{50}{4} - 5$$

$$x = 7.5$$

Option 2

$$\frac{BC}{CD} = \frac{AF}{AC}$$

$$\frac{5}{4} = \frac{10}{x+5}$$

$$x + 5 = 8$$

$$x = 3$$

$x = \underline{7.5}$ or $x = \underline{3}$

# 25 Circle theorems

**Reps**

**1** Find the missing angles in these circles with centre $O$.

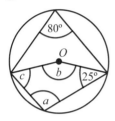 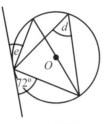 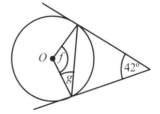

$b = 160°$          $c = 75°$          $d = 72°$

$e = 18°$          $f = 138°$          $g = 21°$

**Exam practice**

**1.** The diagram shows a circle with centre $O$.

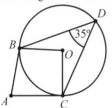

$AB$ and $AC$ are tangents to the circle, and angle $BDC = 35°$.
Find the size of angle $BAC$.
Give a reason for each stage of your working.

$\angle BOC = 70°$ (Angle at centre is twice angle at circumference)
$\angle OBA = \angle OCA = 90°$ (Angle between radius and tangent is 90°)
$\angle BAC + \angle OBA + \angle BOC + \angle OCA = 360°$ (Angles in a quadrilateral add up to 360°)
$\angle BAC = 110°$

**2.** $AC$ is a diameter of the circle with centre $O$. $B$ is a point on the circumference of the circle.

Prove that angle $ABC = 90°$.
You may **not** use any circle theorems in your proof.

Let $\angle OBA = x$ and $\angle OBC = y$
$OB = OC$ because they are both radii
$\angle OAB = x$ and $\angle OCB = y$ (because triangles $OAB$ and $OBC$ are both isosceles)
Therefore $x + x + y + y = 180°$ (angles in triangle $ABC$ add to 180°)
So $x + y = 90°$
So angle $ABC = 90°$

# 26 Vectors

**Reps**

**1** Use the vectors on the right to find $\mathbf{p} = \begin{pmatrix} 2 \\ 6 \end{pmatrix}$ $\mathbf{q} = \begin{pmatrix} 5 \\ 1 \end{pmatrix}$ $\mathbf{r} = \begin{pmatrix} 7 \\ 3 \end{pmatrix}$

**a** $3\mathbf{p} = \begin{pmatrix} 6 \\ 18 \end{pmatrix}$

**b** $\mathbf{q} - \mathbf{r} = \begin{pmatrix} -2 \\ -2 \end{pmatrix}$

**c** $5\mathbf{q} + 2\mathbf{p} = \begin{pmatrix} 29 \\ 17 \end{pmatrix}$

**d** $\frac{1}{2}(\mathbf{q} + \mathbf{r}) = \begin{pmatrix} 6 \\ 2 \end{pmatrix}$

**2** $P$, $R$ and $Q$ are the midpoints of $OA$, $OB$ and $AB$, respectively.
Write in terms of $\mathbf{p}$ and $\mathbf{q}$

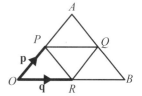

**a** $\overrightarrow{PQ}$    q

**b** $\overrightarrow{BO}$    $-2q$

**c** $\overrightarrow{AO}$    $q - p$

**d** $\overrightarrow{BP}$    $p - 2q$

**Exam practice**

**1.** The vectors $\mathbf{a}$ and $\mathbf{b}$ are defined as $\mathbf{a} = \begin{pmatrix} 10 \\ 8 \end{pmatrix}$ $\mathbf{b} = \begin{pmatrix} 6 \\ k \end{pmatrix}$

Given that $\mathbf{a}$ and $\mathbf{b}$ are parallel, find the value of $k$

$k = \dfrac{6}{10} \times 8 = 4.8$

$k = \underline{4.8}$

**2.**

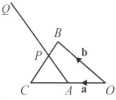

$OCB$ is a triangle. $A$ is the midpoint of $OC$, and $P$ lies on $BC$ such that $CP:PB = 2:1$
$APQ$ is a straight line and $AP:PQ = 1:2$
$\overrightarrow{OA} = \mathbf{a}$ and $\overrightarrow{OB} = \mathbf{b}$
Prove that $QBO$ is a straight line.

$\overrightarrow{OC} = 2\mathbf{a}$

$\overrightarrow{CB} = -\overrightarrow{OC} + \overrightarrow{OB} = \mathbf{b} - 2\mathbf{a}$

$\overrightarrow{CP} = \dfrac{2}{3}\overrightarrow{CB} = \dfrac{2}{3}(\mathbf{b} - 2\mathbf{a})$

$\overrightarrow{AP} = \overrightarrow{AC} + \overrightarrow{CP} = \mathbf{a} + \dfrac{2}{3}(\mathbf{b} - 2\mathbf{a})$

$\overrightarrow{AQ} = 3\overrightarrow{AP} = 2\mathbf{b} - \mathbf{a}$

$\overrightarrow{OQ} = \mathbf{a} + \overrightarrow{AQ} = \mathbf{a} + 2\mathbf{b} - \mathbf{a} = 2\mathbf{b}$

Therefore $OQ$ and $OB$ are parallel and $O$, $B$ and $Q$ are collinear.
So $OBQ$ is a straight line.

# 27 Averages and range

**Reps**

**1** For each set of data values find the mean, the median and the range.

| a | 1.4 | 2.0 | 2.1 | 3.5 | | Mean = 2.25 | Median = 2.05 | Range = 2.1 |
|---|-----|-----|-----|-----|---|-------------|---------------|-------------|
| b | 2 | 2 | 3 | 4 | 8 | 8 | Mean = 4.5 | Median = 3.5 | Range = 6 |
| c | 2 | 7 | 8 | 5 | 5 | | Mean = 5.4 | Median = 5 | Range = 6 |
| d | 10 | 15 | 22 | 13 | | Mean = 15 | Median = 14 | Range = 12 |

**2** This frequency table shows the heights of some plants. Complete the table and find the mean and the class interval which contains the median.

| Height ($h$ cm) | Frequency ($f$) | Midpoint ($x$) | $f \times x$ |
|-----------------|-----------------|----------------|--------------|
| $0 \leqslant h < 10$ | 36 | 5 | $36 \times 5 = 180$ |
| $10 \leqslant h < 20$ | 40 | 15 | $40 \times 15 = 600$ |
| $20 \leqslant h < 30$ | 24 | 25 | $24 \times 25 = 600$ |
| Totals | 100 | | 1380 |

Mean = 13.8 cm    Class interval containing median = $10 \leqslant h < 20$

**Exam practice**

**1.** The frequency table shows the number of trips abroad taken by each member of a class in the last year.

| Number of trips | Frequency | $f \times x$ |
|-----------------|-----------|--------------|
| 0 | 8 | $8 \times 0 = 0$ |
| 1 | 10 | $10 \times 1 = 10$ |
| 2 | 7 | $7 \times 2 = 14$ |
| 3 | 5 | $5 \times 3 = 15$ |
| 4 | 1 | $1 \times 4 = 4$ |
| Total | 31 | 43 |

**(a)** Work out the mean number of trips.

Mean = $\dfrac{43}{31}$ = 1.387...

1.39

**(b)** Work out the median number of trips taken.

16th value is in group for 1 trip

1

**2.** The mean of the following five numbers is 12.6

18    7    $x$    16    $x$

Find the value of $x$.

$18 + 7 + x + 16 + x = 12.6 \times 5$

$41 + 2x = 63$

$2x = 63 - 41$

$2x = 22$

$x = 11$

$x = 11$

# 28 Representing data

**Reps**

**1** Draw a box plot to show the following information about the marks out of 30 scored by students on a test.

| Lowest score | 5 |
| Lower quartile | 11 |
| Median | 20 |
| Upper quartile | 25 |
| Highest score | 29 |

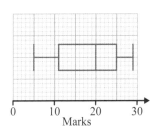

**2** The table shows information about the masses of eggs, from a sample of 50 eggs.

| Mass ($m$ g) | Frequency | Frequency density |
| --- | --- | --- |
| $50 \le m < 60$ | 18 | 1.8 |
| $60 \le m < 70$ | 25 | 2.5 |
| $70 \le m < 80$ | 7 | 0.7 |

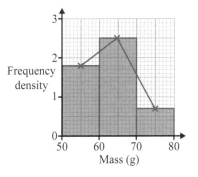

**a** Draw a histogram for this data.

**b** On the same axes, draw a frequency polygon for this data.

**Exam practice**

This cumulative frequency graph shows information about the heights of 120 boys in a sixth form college.

**(a)** Find an estimate for the median height.
167 cm

**(b)** Write true or false for each statement.

**A** The height of the tallest boy was 120 cm. False

**B** The height of the shortest boy was 150 cm. True

**C** More than half the boys were shorter than 170 cm. True

**D** 20 boys were exactly 160 cm tall. False

**(c)** Show that 75% of the boys were shorter than 173 cm.

75% × 120 = 90

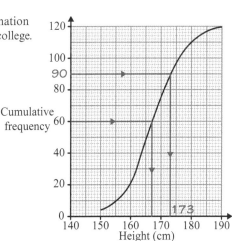

# 29 Probability

**1** A fair six-sided dice is thrown. Find the probability of getting

**a**   an even number    $\frac{3}{6}$

**b**   a square number    $\frac{2}{6}$

**c**   a number less than 6    $\frac{5}{6}$

**d**   a number more than 7    0

**2** A fair coin is tossed three times. Find the probability of getting

**a**   three tails    $\frac{1}{8}$

**b**   exactly two heads    $\frac{3}{8}$

**c**   heads on the first toss    $\frac{1}{2}$

**d**   tails on the first two tosses    $\frac{1}{4}$

**1.** A spinner can land on red or green or blue. The table shows the probabilities of landing on red or green.

| Colour | Red | Green | Blue |
|---|---|---|---|
| Probability | 0.2 | 0.5 | 0.3 |

The spinner is spun once.

**(a)** Work out the probability of landing on blue.

$$\underline{P(Blue) = 0.3}$$

The spinner is spun twice.

**(b)** Work out the probability of landing on the same colour twice.

P(Red-Red) = 0.2 × 0.2 = 0.04
P(Green-Green) = 0.5 × 0.5 = 0.25
P(Blue-Blue) = 0.3 × 0.3 = 0.09
P(same colour) = 0.04 + 0.25 +
              0.09 = 0.38

$$\underset{\ldots\ldots}{0.38}$$

**2.** $\mathcal{E}$ = {prime numbers less than 30}
$A$ = {2, 7, 11, 23}      $B$ = {3, 5, 7}

**(a)** Complete the Venn diagram to show this information.

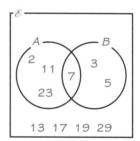

A number is chosen at random from the universal set $\mathcal{E}$.

**(b)** Work out the probability that it is in the set $A \cup B$.

$$P(A \cup B) = \frac{6}{10}$$

$$\underset{\ldots\ldots}{\frac{6}{10}}$$

# 30 Conditional Probability

## Reps

**1** For this Venn diagram, find

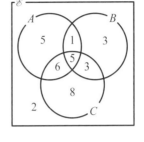

**a** P(A | C)    $\dfrac{11}{22}$

**b** P(B | C)    $\dfrac{8}{22}$

**c** P(A ∩ C | B)    $\dfrac{5}{12}$

**d** P(A ∪ B | C)    $\dfrac{14}{22}$

**2** The probability of a biased coin landing on heads is 0.4
Complete the tree diagram to show the possible outcomes when it is tossed twice.

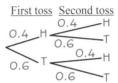

## Exam practice

A box contains 12 red counters and 8 blue counters.
Two counters are picked at random.
Anji draws a probability tree diagram for this information.

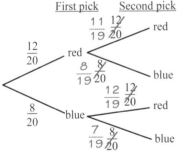

**(a)** Write down **one** thing that is wrong with the probabilities in this tree diagram.

She should have changed the probabilities for the second pick because there will
be 19 counters to choose from, not 20

**(b)** Cross out any incorrect probabilities and write the correct probabilities next to them.

**(c)** Find the probability that the two counters picked are the same colour.

$$\dfrac{12}{20} \times \dfrac{11}{19} + \dfrac{8}{20} \times \dfrac{7}{19} = \dfrac{132 + 56}{380} = \dfrac{188}{380}$$

Published by Pearson Education Limited, 80 Strand, London, WC2R 0RL.

www.pearsonschoolsandfecolleges.co.uk

Copies of official specifications for all Pearson qualifications may be found on the website: qualifications.pearson.com

Text and illustrations © Harry Smith and Pearson Education Ltd 2018
Typeset by Jouve India Private Limited
Produced by Elektra Media Ltd
Cover illustration by Miriam Sturdee

The right of Harry Smith to be identified as author of this work has been asserted by him in accordance with the Copyright, Designs and Patents Act 1988.

First published 2018

24
10 9 8 7 6 5

**British Library Cataloguing in Publication Data**
A catalogue record for this book is available from the British Library

ISBN 978 1 292 24691 8

Printed in Great Britain by Bell and Bain Ltd, Glasgow

**Notes from the publisher**
1. While the publishers have made every attempt to ensure that advice on the qualification and its assessment is accurate, the official specification and associated assessment guidance materials are the only authoritative source of information and should always be referred to for definitive guidance.

   Pearson examiners have not contributed to any sections in this resource relevant to examination papers for which they have responsibility.

2. Pearson has robust editorial processes, including answer and fact checks, to ensure the accuracy of the content in this publication, and every effort is made to ensure this publication is free of errors. We are, however, only human, and occasionally errors do occur. Pearson is not liable for any misunderstandings that arise as a result of errors in this publication, but it is our priority to ensure that the content is accurate. If you spot an error, please do contact us at resourcescorrections@pearson.com so we can make sure it is corrected.